BRITISH
RAILWAYS
ILLUSTRATED

ANNUAL No.13

Welcome to British Railways III

You'll Remember those Black and White Days...

VISIT OUR WEB SITE FOR UP TO DATE INFORMATION ABOUT IRWELL PRESS BOOKS AND MAGAZI

LUSTRATED

ted ANNUAL No.13

Irwell Press brings you all your Christmas favourites for the 13th fabulous year!

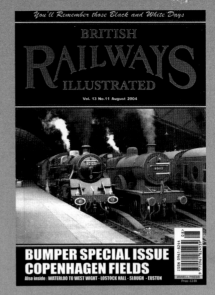

You'll Remember those Black and White Days

BRITISH RAILWAYS ILLUSTRATED
Vol. 13 No.11 August 2004

BUMPER SPECIAL ISSUE COPENHAGEN FIELDS
Also inside : WATERLOO TO WEST WIGHT · LOSTOCK HALL · SLOUGH · EUSTON
Price : £3.99

Pick up a copy of the
monthly magazine
BRITISH RAILWAYS ILLUSTRATED
at a newsagent, specialist book
and model shop or direct from
the publisher every month.
Only £3.30

Cover photograph: Merchant Navy Pacific in original condition; 35019 FRENCH LINE C.G.T. heads the 3.5pm to Waterloo, shortly after leaving Bournemouth West, on 22 May 1950. J.C. Flemons, The Transport Treasury.

Back cover photograph: The Stewarts Lane turntable on 30th January 1954 with Britannia 70014 IRON DUKE. 'The Duke' had only just arrived, six hours late, with the Night Ferry having been delayed by heavy snowfalls in Kent. Philip J. Kelley.

Opposite: framed by a finial, 4094 DYNEVOR CASTLE with a Paddington-Neyland express approaches Llanharan on 14 June 1949. J.C. Flemons, The Transport Treasury.

EDITORIAL MATTERS
Contributions,
submissions, photographs or whatever
(remember the contributor must
address and attend to
copyright), readers'
letters, bouquets
and brickbats for
British Railways Illustrated
must be addressed to Editor,
Chris Hawkins
at 59A, High Street, Clophill,
Bedfordshire MK45 4BE
E-mail chris@irwellpress.co.uk
Tel.01525 861888 or
Fax. 01525 862044
Printed by
The Amadeus Press, Cleckheaton.
Telephone 01274 863210
Copyright:- Irwell Press Ltd. 2004

Diesel-Electric Traction Proposals on the LNER By D.W. Winkworth

The events prefigured in the LNER *Memorandum* of course never took place, which leaves us in the happy position of choosing more or less what we like to illustrate something of what did happen on the LNER's successor, the Eastern, North Eastern and Scottish Regions of BR. Here's a perfect picture of the rejuvenated East Coast services getting under way in the early 1950s, 60003 ANDREW K. McCOSH with the down Capitals Limited, hoisting g the train up Holloway Bank on 7 June 1950. Photograph J.C. Flemons, The Transport Treasury.

You'll Remember those Black and White Days...

You'll Remember those Black and White Days...

For illustrative effect, we have largely chosen the big steam engine aspect of the East Coast route. For many years the A3 class 4-6-2 type monopolised the workings and the sight of a Pacific in King's Cross loco yard was as commonplace as could be. Here 2751 HUMORIST lends a novel touch having been fitted with experimental smoke deflectors. 21 April 1939. Photograph D.W. Winkworth.

TABLE 1
Comparative Data of Steam and Diesel-electric Locomotives

	'Pacific' Locomotive	Locomotive Unit	Double-Unit Locomotive
Wheel formation	4-6-2	6-6	6-6-6-6
Max permissible speed – mph	100	100	100
Total weight in working order – tons	161	120	240
Number of driving axles	3	4	8
Starting tractive effort at 25% adhesion – lb	37,000	40,350	80,700
Tractive effort at 60mph – lb	11,900	6,725	13,450
Tractive effort at 75mph – lb	11,000	6,450	12,900
Length over buffers	73' 2"	57' 0"	114' 0"
Rigid/truck wheel base	14' 6"	15' 0"	15' 0"
Diesel engines	-	one 1600 hp	two 1600 hp
Diesel engine speed rpm	-	750	750

The Diesel-electric tractive effort given does not include amount required for 79 tons additional locomotive weight which is, of course, provided.

The streamlined A4s ousted the A3s from the premier jobs as this picture taken on 24 August 1938 of 4902 SEAGULL, possibly on the 1.30pm down from King's Cross, indicates. Photograph D.W. Winkworth.

In the aftermath of the Second World War the main line railway companies set out their stalls by announcing proposals for the type of traction to be used. Naturally it was more electrification for the Southern augmented by diesel-electric power filling-in between the main routes as well as the possibility of high speed services to the west of England with diesel-electric power. The LMSR went all diesel-electric while the Great Western was its usual idiosyncratic self by opting to explore gas turbine traction.

The LNER, somewhat belatedly, came in last announcing their proposal, in a *Memorandum to the Joint Locomotive and Traffic Committees* dated 24 July 1947. The underlying factor, which prompted this investigation, was the non-availability of steam locomotive power accentuated by the inability to obtain new locomotives either from the company's shops or from contractors. Other problems included the ageing stock requiring an excessive amount of repairs, the shortage and inferior quality of coal.

Non-steam forms of power investigated were main line electrification, gas-turbo-electric locomotives and diesel-electric locomotion. So far as electrification was concerned the drawback was the time factor; for it would take years to convert the whole line between London and Edinburgh when a solution was required in a short time scale. Gas-turbo-electric locomotives, although considered to be suitable if a machine of 3,000 brake horsepower delivered to the generator was available within the loading gauge and on a single underframe, were ruled out because of the amount of development necessary and the time involved.

This left the diesel-electric locomotive with a clear field without prejudicing the eventual adoption of main line electrification should traffic warrant. Accordingly the *Memorandum* devoted itself to the consideration in detail of this type of traction. A condition that had to be faced was that special provision would have to be made for the maintenance of the locomotives. These could not be satisfactorily accommodated alongside steam engines in ordinary running sheds. (A point that BR was slow to take on board years later.) Specially skilled and trained staff would be required for maintaining both diesel engines and the electric traction

TABLE 2
Trains to be covered by means of 25 locomotive units

	Weekdays	Sundays
Edinburgh to King's Cross	10.0am	11.15am
	10.15am	11.25am
	1.10pm	7.50pm
	7.50pm	9.30pm
	9.30pm (SX)	10.0pm
	10.0pm	10.20pm
	10.20pm	10.40pm
	10.40pm	
King's Cross to Edinburgh	1.0am	11.0am
	9.45am	11.20am
	10.0am	7.5pm
	1.0pm	7.30pm
	7.5pm (SX)	
	7.30pm	
	8.20pm (SO)	
	10.15pm	10.15pm
	10.30pm	10.30pm

In addition, the following trains have been included in order to provide for the full employment of the Diesel-electric locomotive units in traffic:-

	Weekdays	Sundays
Aberdeen to Edinburgh	9.10am	
Doncaster to King's Cross	1.32pm	
Grantham to King's Cross	1.21pm	12.58pm
Edinburgh to Aberdeen	3.40am	
King's Cross to Doncaster	8.55am	
King's Cross to Grantham	9.15am	10.0am

Total train mileage – 2,460,000 (approx) per annum

equipment on a routine basis. The introduction of diesel-electric tractive units would mean that there would be nothing more than replacement of one form of independent locomotive by another thus obviating special coaching stock such as railcars being required.

A full scale example of a particular and important group of passenger services would demonstrate the capacity for continuous operation without refuelling or other attention over much longer distances than steam locomotives. It was on the East Coast passenger services that the most comprehensive trial could be made. The trailing load of these trains was taken as 520 tons for which two locomotive units of 1,600 brake horsepower giving a total of 3,200 brake horsepower equivalent to 2,400 rail horsepower at the driving wheels and operated by multiple-unit control would be required. Comparative particulars of a Pacific steam locomotive and a double unit diesel-electric locomotive are given in Table 1.

A scheme providing for the operation of diesel-electric traction of the principal trains in each direction between London and Edinburgh including a total passenger train mileage of approximately 3,460,000 annually had been drawn up. The services concerned as detailed in Table 2 would require ten double-unit locomotives in traffic. A total stock of 25 single units would be required (allowing for overhaul and maintenance periods). These 25 units would displace 26 Pacifics in traffic (or 32 engines in the stock). It was rather different from BR's later '22 Deltics for 55 Pacifics' equation.

Separate and specialised maintenance accommodation would be essential, which would be best arranged with a main depot at or near one terminus with a subsidiary depot at or near the other terminus. A suitable site for the main depot was to be found at Leith Central, two miles from Edinburgh Waverley station, affording housing for four or five double-unit locomotives. The subsidiary depot would be at either Finsbury Park goods yard or Holloway cattle sidings. The proposed facilities are shown in Table 3.

The *Memorandum* next turned to comparative costs. The compilers were handicapped inasmuch as there was no equivalent British data which could be used and much recourse had to be made to American figures, which did not necessarily run parallel to home practice. So estimates tended to be 'guesstimates' of a glossy nature putting the best interpretations forward. Again, a presage of events to come.

During the war, as is well known, the side valances were removed from the A4s. These had tended to give a 'long skirt' look to the engines and with them gone a fleet look was introduced as demonstrated by 60004 WILLIAM WHITELAW drawing into Berwick-upon-Tweed with the up morning Talisman on 4 August 1951. Photograph D.W. Winkworth.

TABLE 3
Proposed maintenance facilities for Diesel-electric locomotives
MAIN DEPOT – EDINBURGH
1 It is proposed that the main maintenance depot for diesel-electric locomotives for the Anglo-Scottish services should be provided in part of Leith Central Station, 2 miles from Edinburgh Waverley.
2 The depot would be obtained by using the sidings at the south side of Leith Central together with parts of nos 1 and 2 platforms. Covered accommodation approximately 250 feet long and 120 feet wide would be provided, capable of housing 4 or 5 double-unit diesel-electric locomotives. The site is easy of access by road and rail and the accommodation proposed is capable of extension in the future if required.
3 Siding accommodation would be available for the standage of additional units adjacent to the covered accommodation and for the handling of stores and materials.
4 Two 30-ton overhead travelling cranes, platforms, inspection pits, machine shop, oil fuelling installation and staff accommodation would be provided.
5 The cost would be approximately £200,000.
6 The performance elsewhere of certain work now performed at Leith Central would require to be further considered if the diesel-electric proposal were proceeded with.

SUBSIDIARY DEPOT – LONDON
7 The subsidiary depot at the London end should be as near as King's Cross as possible, to keep to the minimum the movement of diesel-electric locomotives through an area already congested. Possible sites exist at Finsbury Park Goods Yard and Holloway Cattle Sidings.
8 The facilities to be provided would include two 30-ton overhead travelling cranes (for emergency lifts in case a double-unit locomotive could not be worked back to the Main Depot), inspection pits, platforms and oil fuelling installation.
9 The site selected would have to be capable of extension to meet future increased needs, and the estimated costs of providing the accommodation immediately required is £60,000.

For fuel costs general estimates were made. The overall thermo-dynamic efficiency from fuel to rail was steam 6 per cent and for diesel-electric 24 per cent; fuel consumption for a trailing load of 520 tons from King's Cross to Edinburgh (393 miles) was 10.52 tons for coal (based on 60lb per train mile) and 2.10 tons in the case of diesel-electric (12lb of fuel oil per train mile). The fuel costs per train mile King's Cross to Edinburgh was put at 12.84d (based on coal costing £2 per ton) and for diesel-electric 10.28d (based on fuel oil costing £8 per ton).

Construction costs were based on British currency at the end of 1945. For a 1,500hp diesel-electric locomotive unit the costing was £31,250 rising to £45,000 for a 2,000 hp unit. The American rule of thumb reckoning was that the diesel units were approximately double the cost of a steam locomotive of like power. The LNER had found out, as had the LMSR and SR, that there was but one British contractor building diesel-electric locomotives for main line working, with the most powerful in the 1,600 hp range. This would necessitate the operation of two units per train to obtain a required figure of 3,200 hp following the big engine policy favoured by the LNER.

It was estimated, at 1947 prices, that the proposed diesel-electric fleet would cost £1,127,500. The diesel engines and electric traction equipment would cost £36,000 per unit with mechanical parts being built at Doncaster (at £130 per ton) costing £9,100 per unit. For 32 Pacifics required to work the services the total construction cost would be £512,000.

To the cost of the 25 units there would be added the facilities in Leith and London costed at £260,000 giving a rounded-up total cost of £1,390,000, so making the diesel-electric scheme approximately £880,000 more expensive than steam.

The estimated total operating costs covering depreciation, general overhaul and repairs, inspection and running maintenance and train working costs (including wages and fuel) was summarised, on the basis of 2,460,000 miles per annum as laid out in the table at the top of page 9.

A summary of conclusions gathered up the arguments set forth for each facet of the proposal and added further remarks such as the ratio of operating costs being 100 per cent for steam and 92.2 per cent for diesel-electric and the cost of imported oil (the debacle of conversion from coal to oil and reconversion had yet to come!). Advantages cited were increased traction availability, higher acceleration and better performances on adverse gradients,

A4 class 60021 WILD SWAN hoots at the photographer as it overtakes an up local train near Brookmans Park on 8 July 1958 with the up Elizabethan. Photograph D.W. Winkworth.

You'll Remember those Black and White Days...

	Steam	**Diesel-electric**
Depreciation	£9600	£46200
General overhaul and repairs	£64000	£43800
Inspection/running m'tenance	£38400	£25000
Train working costs:		
Footplatemen	£65800	£67800
Fuel	£131600	£105400
Fuel handling etc	£5000	£2000

These added up to £314,400 for steam at 30.7d per train mile and £290,200 (28.3d) for diesel-electric.

Below. Post-war and the A1 class as designed by the Peppercorn has come into the reckoning. 60117 BOIS ROUSSEL heads the down Queen of Scots near Stevenage on 14 October 1957. Photograph D.W. Winkworth.

Edinburgh Waverley with the 5.45pm train to Berwick leaving in charge of A1 class 60129 GUY MANNERING on 15 July 1962. Photograph D.W. Winkworth.

You'll Remember those Black and White Days...

60132 MARMION of the A1 class entering Peterborough North bound for King's Cross. This was 30 May 1955 when the disastrous rail strike was in its second day. Photograph D.W. Winkworth.

cleanliness and publicity and prestige value. The *Memorandum* concluded:

'It is therefore RECOMMENDED:-
(i) that the experiment on the lines set out with 25 diesel-electric locomotive units in replacement of 32 'Pacific' steam locomotives be

approved in principle; and
(ii) that enquiries be made of all possible builders of diesel-electric locomotives and designs and quotations obtained'.

It was signed by Miles Beevor although it would appear that C.P. Hopkins (later to go to the Southern

Region of BR) had a large hand in its preparation. It is now history how the East Coast line not only got big diesel-electric engines in the Deltics but also went on to enjoy electrification all as suggested in this document.

60121   SILURIAN certainly has a big engine look about it as it passes through Selby on 24 July 1961 with the 9.30am Glasgow-King's Cross   service. Photograph   D.W. Winkworth.

You'll Remember those Black and White Days...

You'll Remember those Black and White Days...

They didn't come any larger than this, the rebuilt 4-6-2-2 (or 4-6-4) W class 60700 known in pre-war days as 10000. Here it is approaching Welwyn North with an up Hull express on 15 April 1953. Perhaps its very size (it was longer than an A4) could be a stumbling block. The cylinders were 20in by 26in as compared with the 18½in by 26in of the A4s and the grate area was advanced from 41¼sq ft to 50 sq ft, which would keep the fireman busy especially as there was no coal-pusher fitted. Photograph D.W. Winkworth.

And wouldn't the V2 2-6-2 Green Arrow class qualify as a big engine? Here an unidentified member of the class shows off its lines on a down express just north of Doncaster on 23 May 1959. Photograph D.W. Winkworth.

You'll Remember those Black and White Days...

It was surely no accident that the *Memorandum* foresaw 'single locomotive units' of 1,600hp, for this was the size then under development by Ivatt with English Electric as the LMS 'Twins', 10000 and 10001. So this is what the LNER fleet might have looked like – the original at Bletchley with a northbound train, on 21 May 1960. Photograph Frank Hornby.

Oddly, the actuality of diesel provision on the East Coast was, if anything more a matter of the provision of *small* diesel locomotives – like the ill-starred 'Baby Deltics' as illustrated by D5909 at King's Cross suburban side on 26 November 1960. Photograph Frank Hornby.

Some of the thinking in the *Memorandum* survived in the choice of depots and Finsbury Park was duly chosen at the end of the 1950s for London – here it is nearing completion in February 1960, incorporating all the fancy aids such as raised walkways and working levels.

Talk of large East Coast locos and dieselisation must of course lead to the Deltics – such as newly outshopped D9001 at where else but EE's Vulcan Foundry in 1961.

You'll Remember those Black and White Days...

The Farnborough Flyer

The Farnborough Flyer flew under an arrangement made by Mr Alan Pegler, well-known for the 'Northern Rubber Specials' of the period and the subsequent preservation of FLYING SCOTSMAN. He it was who organised The Flyer, on Sunday 12 September 1954 (for his fellow members of the Royal Observer Corps) to view the Farnborough Air Show. The Great Northern Atlantic No.251 was used, assisted by Director 4-4-0 62663 PRINCE ALBERT, an engine unfortunately 'slated for early condemnation' as the *Trains Illustrated* report put it. A B1 worked the train from Leeds to Doncaster where a 'Flying Scotsman' buffet lounge and one of the 'Coronation' beaver tail observation cars were added. 251 and 62663 duly took over, running to Basingstoke via Retford, Mansfield, Leicester, Banbury, Oxford, Didcot and Reading. From there an SR Mogul took the train on to the Show at Farnborough while the engines and

observation car were serviced at Basingstoke shed. To get the same order of vehicles for the return, the rest of the train was taken by a pair of SR 2-6-0s on a circuit to Virginia Water, Ascot and Camberley while the passengers enjoyed the show. The Director and the GN Atlantic were re-attached at Basingstoke and: *ended the day with a rollicking 75mph down the hill, running the 23.4 miles from Leicester to Nottingham, a severe slack near Wilford Road included, in under 28 minutes.* Left-hand page: the visitors pose in turn with one of the 'locals', Schools 4-4-0 30901 WINCHESTER while this page shows them being serviced along with King Arthurs (top) 30751 ETARRE and (below) 30745 TINTAGEL. The beaver tail car is already turned for the journey. Photographs Les Elsey

You'll Remember those Black and White Days...

Under The Pennines At Woodhead ('Bridge 70C') Bryan Wilson

The Sheffield, Ashton-Under-Lyne and Manchester Railway formally opened the first Woodhead Tunnel, a single line of 3 miles and 22 chains, on 22 December 1845, with public use commencing the day after. The original plans were for two tracks but, then as now, economy dictated the outcome. It was at that time the longest tunnel in the country and a pilot locomotive was attached as authority for trains to pass through.

As traffic levels grew, as early as 1847 an additional line of rails through the Pennines was seen as essential and work started on a second bore. This was duly opened on 2 February 1852 by the Manchester, Sheffield & Lincolnshire Railway.

A hundred years of continuous use by steam locomotives took its toll and, by 1946, weekend engineering possessions were inadequate to keep pace with the rate of deterioration; indeed, nine months of 'Single Line Working' on each line with some services diverted still did not allow engineers to accomplish the outstanding work.

Early in BR days, in fact on 15 November 1948, the Railway Executive authorised the construction of a third tunnel with work starting in February 1949. The main contractors were Balfour, Beatty & Co. This was to be a new

double line bore together with the necessary remodelling at Woodhead and Dunford Bridge stations. This meant new platforms, station buildings and signal boxes at both places, a new overbridge at Dunford and a new river bridge across the Etherow at Woodhead. Some housing at Dunford Bridge was demolished and had to be replaced and new station masters' houses were built at both places.

Electrification of the route was approved between Manchester, Sheffield and Wath by the LNER in 1936 and work started, only to be suspended in 1939 for the duration of the Second World War. When completed, the new tunnel became the third largest on BR, at 3 miles 66 chains, after the Severn and the Totley. Interestingly, the summit of the line was now actually in the tunnel instead of where it used to be, at Dunford Bridge.

No steam train used the new tunnel which meant ordinary Portland cement could be used for lining. The concreting was actually completed on 26 June 1953. One track had to be laid by hand but, as our pictures show, the other could be put down using a track laying machine. The tunnel was complete in October 1953 and cost about four and a quarter million pounds. It was electrically lit throughout and both lines were signalled for two way

working to ease maintenance arrangements. On 13 June 1954 the tracks at each end were connected to the new alignment and the old Woodhead tunnels were in railway use no more. The later sad decline to eventual closure in 1981 is well documented but let us look at more optimistic days in three views of 'Bridge 70C' under construction.

Above. **Looking through the Tunnel in 1953 with one track only, which has been laid by hand. The square-looking hole up in the roof on the right is for the steel boom of the overhead electric traction equipment which will be mounted on a bracket in this recess. The attachments to the walls are for the cables supplying electricity to traction sub-stations, also linking supply points in Lancashire and Yorkshire. Additionally there is space for the sub-station supervisory control cable. On the other side, the attachments are to carry six signal and telecommunications cables, including one for the 24 emergency telephones, located in recesses in the tunnel at 220 yard intervals.**

WOODHEAD NEW TUNNEL
LENGTH 3 MILES 66 YARDS

OPENED BY
THE R.T. HON. ALAN LENNOX-BOYD P.C. M.P.
MINISTER OF TRANSPORT AND CIVIL AVIATION
THURSDAY 3rd JUNE 1954

J.J.CAMPBELL M.I.C.E. CIVIL ENGINEER, EASTERN REGION, BRITISH RAILWAYS
SIR WILLIAM HALCROW & PARTNERS M.I.C.E CONSULTING ENGINEERS
BALFOUR BEATTY & COMPANY LIMITED CIVIL ENGINEERING CONTRACTORS

PLAQUE AT WOODHEAD PORTAL

You'll Remember those Black and White Days...

Diesel shunter No.12105 stands beside the 'pre-fab' train in the new tunnel in the summer of 1953. 12105 had gone to Mexborough (with 12103 and 12104 and new D3060 and D3061) in August that year for work at Wath Yard. Track laying in the tunnel was completed by 1 October so that ties the date down fairly well. Although an Eastern Region project, the pre-fab wagon belongs to the Civil Engineer Watford – if the stencilling on the solebar is anything to go by.

A 'Trilby Hat' watches 12105 and its attendant machinery as more track is manoeuvred into place while that in the foreground awaits ballast for completion. The Track Laying machine was 'No.2 Unit from Bletchley Depot' again betraying an LMR interest long before the tunnel became LM territory.

You'll Remember those Black and White Days...

Hazy Days

The air in London thins under sustained sunlight to a sort of dry asphalt vapour, though it would be hard to say if in the 1950s it was actually worse. 'Down in the loco' at Camden it could certainly look bad as steam and dust in the sun and breeze imparted a thin, hazy look to the place. Thus Camden's very own 46240 CITY OF COVENTRY, ready for the Mid-Day Scot, appears to fade into the haze on 9 August 1953. These are the ash pits at the north end of the shed. One of the shed's 'Jocko' 3F tanks stands behind and beyond is 46252 CITY OF LEICESTER. Below is a closer view of CITY OF LEICESTER, up in London from its home shed Carlisle Upperby (then 12A). Right in the same haze and on the same day is 46239 CITY OF CHESTER, piled high with coal and ready top back down to Euston. Photographs A.R. Carpenter, The Transport Treasury.

You'll Remember those Black and White Days...

Redoubtable WD

You'll Remember those Black and White Days...

We're more accustomed, in the pages of *British Railways Illustrated* to miserable, filthy, bedraggled WDs, wheezing and limping ('Pity the Poor WD', various issues) but, as is apparent from these jolly views, they could look good enough when fresh from works. Here is one of New England's complement, for long used on the endless London coal trains, enjoying an afternoon out at Potters Bar with 'train 1123', a pick-up goods, on 16 June 1951. It would have left New England yard about 8 o'clock in the morning, one of a succession of pick-ups that would 'work' the main line during the day. 'Odd' numbers in the Working Timetable meant an up working and 'even' numbers a down working. 'No.1123' would call at most yards and sidings on the line, all the way to Ferme Park, Hornsey; the job might take 8-10 hours and the WD might see three separate crews during the course of a day's work. Has the bolt detail on the leading edge of a WD front truck *ever* been seen before? Photographs J.C. Flemons, The Transport Treasury.

You'll Remember those Black and White Days...

By Steam and Diesel to Melrose
Robert M. Grogans

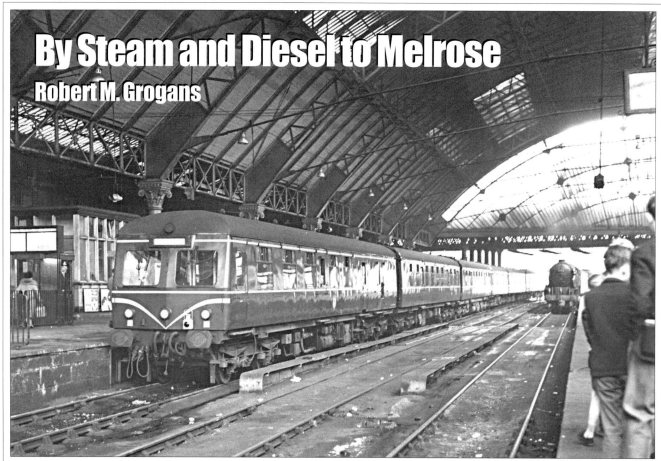

Despite the revolutionary impact of the diesel sets, turnround times retained more than a whiff of steam operating – this is a pair of three car Swindon 'Cross-Country' sets, waiting at Glasgow Queen Street at 11.25 to form the 12.10 departure for Edinburgh Waverley on 13 May 1961. An A2, 60530 SAYAJIRAO, is arriving with a parcels train. Photograph Michael Mensing.

Picture the scene. A March Saturday morning in 1960 and a stiff spring breeze swirled around as a six-car BR green liveried, Swindon-built DMU exited the Queen Street tunnel on the Cowlairs incline, a punishing 1 in 42. It provided the 10.30 a.m. Saturdays-only service, with buffet car, between Glasgow Queen Street and Edinburgh Waverley. The former North British Glasgow to Edinburgh line was one of the first Scottish cross country inter-city routes to be regularly served by the diesel units and it was the writer's first journey on a set between Scotland's two major cities.

The haul up the Cowlairs incline was accompanied by the diesel engine's steadily increased pitch, like a louder version of a car engine as the gears are dropped to enable the vehicle to climb a particularly steep hill. With some of the small air vent type windows at the top of the larger main windows opened to get rid of stale air, the staccato-like sound of the diesel engine reverberated from the tunnel roof and walls.

With the steady introduction from 1957 of diesel services from Glasgow Queen Street the need for bankers to assist the steam services out of the station had gradually declined. (Back in the deeps of time a cable

hauled system had been developed, whereby the train locomotive was assisted up the incline by means of a wire rope attached to the engine and operated from a point at the summit of the incline, near to Cowlairs station in the city's Springburn district.)

It was easy to imagine that Cowlairs station had been built to provide trains with a chance to pause fleetingly before moving on to start the main part of their journey. In the heart of Glasgow's main steam locomotive engine manufacturing district I was able to take in the view from the diesel car window as the DMU passed through the empty Cowlairs platforms. We then headed out of the city into the comfortably established outer suburb of Bishopbriggs, domicile of the wealthier and professional class of Glasgow citizen.

The 10.30 a.m. did not stop at either Cowlairs or Bishopbriggs, but shortly after having picked up speed from the latter, the DMU started to slow before it crept through Lenzie, a station that served an older version of Bishopbriggs. A quiet place, I was sure it would not be unlike my destination, the Scottish border town of Melrose.

The journey to Melrose was not only my first trip on a DMU but would also be my first experience of travel

on the historic Edinburgh-Carlisle Waverley route. Much of it ran through the romantic and spectacularly beautiful Scottish Border country, so beloved of the nineteenth century novelist Sir Walter Scott. I was headed to visit my brother and his wife, recently married and settled in Melrose.

Thoughts of Melrose soon disappeared as the DMU sped from Lenzie and travelled over the junction with the branch line to Kirkintilloch. It then raced through the stations for the villages of Croy, an old settlement of coal miners and quarry workers, and Dullatur, a small hamlet populated by wealthy professionals such as surgeons and solicitors and comfortably retired individuals. It then cut speed through Castlecary station on the western end of the Castlecary viaduct. This carries the line over the cutting of the A80 dual carriageway, snaking northwards toward Stirling. Just a few hundred yards north, the Forth and Clyde canal runs parallel with the viaduct and the landscape generally flattens out as roads, railway and canal cut through the Kelvin Valley or what has often been called the 'waistline of Scotland'.

When the line was constructed in the early 1840s it was kept as level as possible, but that required overcoming several obstacles. These included the construction of the Castlecary and the Almond Water viaducts (the latter a superb 36-arch structure), a mile-long cut through hard rock at Croy ridge, and tunnels at Falkirk, Winchburgh and at the entrances to Queen Street and Waverley stations.

Castlecary station, like Dullatur, has long since succumbed to the machinations of a certain Dr. Beeching, but such disasters were far from a teenage mind that day in 1960. The train soon eased away and travelled over the viaduct. Within a few minutes it had crossed a less elaborate bridge, below which the main line north to Stirling, Perth and Inverness ran through the landscape.

The DMU briefly hurtled through the countryside before it slowed slightly as it passed through Bonnybridge High station. Another victim of Beeching, it was a typical small sleepy Scottish town where apparently nothing ever happened, until a series of alleged UFO-related incidents in the early 1990s threatened to give it an American Roswell-style status.

Shortly after Bonnybridge, the industrial conurbation in and around Falkirk blanked out the rural vistas that had dominated the journey since the train had left the suburbs of Glasgow. At 10.55 a.m. Falkirk High was the first stop on

the trip. After that it paused briefly at 11.02 a.m. at Polmont before it headed for Manuel where it passed non-stop. The latter was the junction link to the mining town and small port of Borrowstouness, always abbreviated to Bo'ness in the modern day. Manuel station has long since been a memory, but the line from it to Bo'ness is still there, now single track and operated as a preserved railway under the auspices of the Scottish Railway Preservation Society.

After Manuel the six car unit again gathered speed to race through the flat landscape before entering at 11.10 a.m. the historic town of Linlithgow with its ruined palace. It had once seen many a Scottish aristocratic intrigue, some of which involved the tragic Mary, Queen of Scots.

Just as it is today, Linlithgow was the last stop before Haymarket on the western edge of Edinburgh's famed Princes Street. However, in previous years a quartet of stations had existed before Haymarket was reached, two of which, Philipstoun and Winchburgh, were small settlements on the eastern stretch of the route between Linlithgow and Edinburgh. After that, within Edinburgh's western suburbs, were Ratho and Gogar.

By 1960 the Glasgow-Edinburgh service raced non-stop from Linlithgow, passed over the junction

for the line to the Forth Bridge and the county of Fife, and soon entered Edinburgh with the hill overlooking the city, romantically named Arthur's seat, rising in the distance. Haymarket sheds were passed and then the large building with the 'Jenners' sign indicating the storage base for the famed Edinburgh department store – the Scottish capital's version of 'Harrods'.

After a brief stop at 11.30 a.m. at Haymarket station the DMU entered first the Haymarket and then the Mound tunnels and at 11.35 a.m. slowed to a halt at Edinburgh Waverley station in the shadow of the volcanic plug at the top of which stands Edinburgh Castle.

The journey had taken an hour and five minutes and there followed nearly an hour and a half before the Edinburgh Waverley-Hawick stopper service departed at 12.52 p.m. Again that was a Saturdays-only service, and it saved the need to make a dash for an earlier service which left before midday. Cue a welcome and relaxed visit to the large station cafeteria and a perusal of the newspaper and magazine kiosk to pick up one of O.S. Nock's famed railway books, by then published in more affordable paperback editions.

The Hawick service was a complete change from the trip from Glasgow. As it awaited its passengers at the platforms on the eastern approaches to Waverley, a

One of the N15/1 0-6-2Ts used to bank trains up to Cowlairs stand from Glasgow Queen Street on 13 May 1961, ready for the off with the up Queen of Scots Pullman. Photograph Michael Mensing.

You'll Remember those Black and White Days...

B1 4-6-0 gently steamed, its blackened bodywork in contrast to the five much cleaner maroon liveried corridor coaches.

Spot on the departure time of 12.52 p.m. the train gently headed out of the station. It was suddenly strange to be alone in a corridor coach compartment, a far cry from the open plan of the DMU and the surrounding beat of the diesels. The chug of the steam engine in the distance as it gradually accelerated was accompanied by the various creaks and groans of the coach's seat springs and metalwork, working in harmony as speed picked up.

The Waverley route through the Lothian and Borders country had often been described as a twisting, winding railway which in addition had two testing ascents and descents, at Fala and Whitrope. The overall effect of the twists and turns and the hill climbs and descents was to restrict the speed of the trains, even the express services, and also determined the type of steam engine that could successfully negotiate these various obstacles. It was certainly a contrast from the Glasgow-Edinburgh part of the journey.

The writer's father, a lifelong railway worker, travelled the line on a number of occasions and often ridiculed what he considered the pedestrian pace of the local passenger services. He was blissfully unaware of the physical and geographic restrictions that were imposed upon the drivers and their hard working firemen. The train passed through Abbeyhill and Piershill stations without stopping and gradually increased speed on its way to the first stop at Portobello. That romantically named suburb of Edinburgh had a large stretch of sandy beach, and even in 1960 still attracted family holidaymakers in the days before the sand and sangria of Spain became more accessible and popular.

From Portobello the line turned back inland in a south-easterly direction through Niddrie and Millerhill. The latter became the centre of a huge goods complex in the days when railway freight traffic was still of widely varied and voluminous proportions. The next stop was Eskbank where any intending passengers for the mining town of Dalkeith alighted. The running time to Eskbank was just over sixteen minutes and about five minutes later the B1 (its number is lost in time, I'm afraid) was pulling its train over the viaduct at Newtongrange and into the mining town's station. The main pit in the town was the Lady Victoria Colliery, which nowadays has been preserved and developed into the Scottish Mining Museum. Now a suburb for commuters for Edinburgh, in 1960 Newtongrange was one of the leading coal mining centres in the Lothians.

Newtongrange was soon left behind as the Hawick-bound service made for the next station on the line, at Gorebridge. It took about six minutes, though the distance was about the same as from Eskbank to Newtongrange. The first hints were coming of an increasingly steadier gradient. The climb up Falahill from Gorebridge took over twelve minutes, and the B1 could be heard labouring hard en route to the summit. A few minutes from Gorebridge the site of the former Fushiebridge station was passed and as the landscape became more desolate the numbers of sheep increased – for centuries this country had been ideal sheep grazing ground.

Tynehead station was passed ten minutes or so out of Gorebridge, a welcome marker no doubt for the engine crew as they prepared for the last push to the summit of Falahill. Tynehead was about three miles up Borthwick Bank which commenced shortly after Fushiebridge, a 1 in 70 gradient which peaked about a mile out of Tynehead. The locomotive could almost be heard giving a sigh

N15/1 0-6-2T 69138 at Queen Street. The notable feature of these tanks of course was the slip coupling for detaching themselves from the banked train – note the pulley on the near side of the smokebox. Several were rostered each day from Eastfield shed, worked as a separate link of thirty men who were very much senior to those in other pilot links. Photograph The Transport Treasury.

You'll Remember those Black and White Days...

Two three car Swindon 'Cross Country' sets arriving at Glasgow Queen Street with the 10am from Edinburgh Waverley, 14 May 1960. On the left is one of the 'Intercity' sets, in its turn bound for Edinburgh. Photograph Michael Mensing.

A Swindon-built 'Intercity' set, forming the 4.40pm Edinburgh Waverley to Glasgow Queen Street, arrives at Bonnybridge High on 1 August 1959. The station closed in 1967 and little trace remains. Photograph W.A.C. Smith.

You'll Remember those Black and White Days...

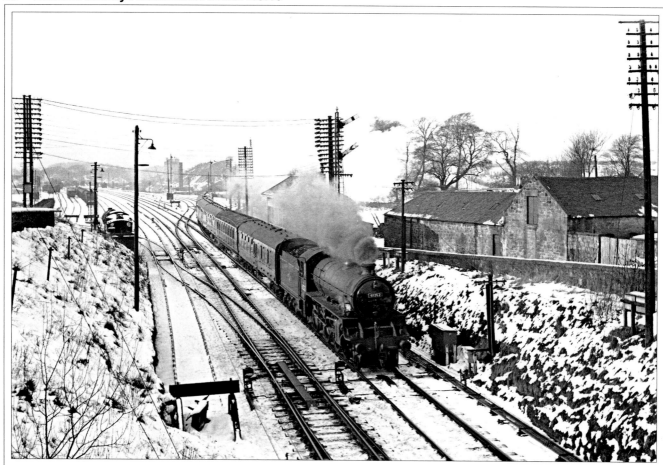

In wintry conditions B1 4-6-0 61262 comes off the Falkirk-Grahamston line at Polmont Junction with the 12.35pm from Glasgow Buchanan Street to Kirkcaldy, 20 January 1960. Photograph W.A.C. Smith.

A2 60536 TRIMBUSH leaves Polmont with the down 'North Briton' Leeds to Glasgow Queen Street on 20 January 1960. The Metro-Cammell twin is forming the 2.39pm connection to Falkirk Grahamston. Photograph W.A.C. Smith.

Above. J37 0-6-0 64570 removes the failed 4.40pm Edinburgh Waverley to Glasgow Queen Street from Polmont on 7 May 1960. The Intercity set had been pushed into the station by A4 60011 EMPIRE OF INDIA with the 5.15pm from Edinburgh which eventually resumed its journey 50 minutes late. The diesel's return working at 6.30pm from Queen Street was taken by B1 61342. Photograph W.A.C. Smith.

of relief as it started the descent from Fala summit on its way to the then important Borders railway town of Galashiels.

On reaching Fala summit, the distance travelled from Edinburgh Waverley had been eighteen miles and had taken some forty minutes of at times very hard steaming. Just over a mile from the summit the train cruised into Heriot station. From Heriot the journey was much quicker with an average speed double that since Gorebridge had been left behind. Thereafter came stops at Fountainhall and Stow stations. Fountainhall had once been junction for the Lauder light railway, closed in 1932.

Stow was a typical Borders mill town, or more accurately large village, and in 1960 was the last station before Galashiels. Some years before there had been a

station at Bowland between Stow and Galashiels, near to the Bowland tunnel, but it had closed due to lack of traffic.

Between Edinburgh Waverley and Newtongrange no fewer than four junctions had been crossed and before Galashiels came a fifth, Kilnknowe Junction. It was the southern point at which trains serving the Edinburgh Waverley-Galashiels via Peebles line entered onto or exited from the Waverley route as they made their way to and from Galashiels.

The run down from Falahill had seen the Gala Water, a feeder for the River Tweed, criss-crossed on several occasions, and it was quite a shock when that idyllic rural scene was ended. Parts of Galashiels were semi-industrial with many woollen mills, together with a railway clutter of engine sheds, goods yard, and busy passenger station. The train paused at Galashiels for about three minutes and then headed on to the writer's destination, Melrose, the next stop.

Melrose station was entered some seven minutes out of Galashiels. After an hour and twenty minutes travel from Edinburgh Waverley, the B1 steamed out of the station, the smoke curling

around the buildings that housed the ticket office and sundry other railway premises such as the porters and waiting rooms.

Preserved as a listed building, these old premises still exist, although now they serve as a gourmet-style restaurant. The platform is also still there but, tragically from a rail enthusiast's point of view, it now looks on to the busy by-pass road that has been constructed over parts of the railway in and around the town.

In 1960 Melrose was a popular stop-over for holiday and tourist traffic in the south-east Scottish Borders and during the summer months the station was busy with such traffic. It finally closed in 1969 and while the area is still a popular tourist destination the lack of a rail service has only added to the pressures on what is still predominantly a rural road system.

The following Sunday evening, at 7.05 p.m. the writer caught his return stopper from Hawick to Edinburgh Waverley hauled by a BR 4MT 2-6-4T, in charge of just four corridor coaches. It was windy and raining steadily and the poor light soon hastened darkness with the result that the sights of the previous day were soon blotted out. For virtually the entire trip home to

Glasgow, where I arrived exactly three hours after departure from Melrose, filthy March weather and darkness soon had me glad that I had purchased Nock's reprinted *Scottish Railways*. He was to be envied that his trip over the Waverley from Edinburgh to Carlisle was on the footplate of A3 Pacific 60067 LADAS which hauled nine coaches.

My trip was carried out at the beginning of an era of change on British Railways. Diesel power was making steady inroads into the Scottish rail system but on routes such as the Waverley, though diesel power had made an appearance (particularly with the Edinburgh-Galashiels via Peebles service) steam was still in charge. Within a few years that had changed with steam all but gone from most routes. Worse, some nine years on, both passenger and freight services on the Waverley had ceased altogether and the Scottish south-east border country was entirely denuded of rail transport, save for the east coast main line to England.

A bus link between Galashiels and Carlisle has operated for many years, giving access for Borders travellers who wish to use the west coast main line services to the north and south. A poor substitute for the once abundant Borders rail network and services. On that March 1960 journey no fewer than seventeen stations stopped at or passed through have since been closed, along with one entire route and its branch lines. Given the picturesque setting and the rich historical past of the Scottish Borders, it is a crying shame that railway preservation never developed in the area, as indeed it has in other equally picturesque parts of the British mainland.

Six car original Swindon Intercity unit forming the 1.30pm from Glasgow Queen Street, arriving at Edinburgh Waverley on 22 May 1962. It had been recognised as far back as GWR days that fast diesel sets were ideal for main line services of a more modest distance. The three car sets had 'intermediate' driving cars with centre gangway connections. The Glasgow-Edinburgh route was picked out as the obvious route to benefit from such services as early as 1952 (see 'British Rail Fleet Survey 8' by Brian Haresnape, Ian Allan 1985) and trials were recommended by the BTC. So it was that even before the BR Modernisation Plan was announced Swindon began the design work for the 'Intercity' sets. Photograph Michael Mensing.

The far from inspiring 'flat' front end of the Scottish Intercity units provided from Swindon were distinctive, if dull. Oddly, there were no marker lights, or destination blind – just this crude illuminated 'A' denoting express passenger. The term 'Intercity' predated the later BR term which came to indicate express passenger services in general. The driver reads his paper in car Sc79096 as it waits at Waverley on 22 May 1962 to form the 1pm to Glasgow Queen Street. Photograph Michael Mensing.

Former Western Region Britannia Pacific 70018 FLYING DUTCHMAN leaves Melrose with the 1.28pm from Carlisle to Edinburgh Waverley on 25 September 1961. Photograph W.A.C. Smith.

A3 Pacific 60093 CORONACH, a long-time resident at Carlisle Canal shed, arrives at Melrose with the 2.36pm from Edinburgh Waverley to Carlisle on 25 September 1961. Photograph W.A.C. Smith.

B1 4-6-0 61341 crosses the twenty-two arch Newbattle viaduct over the River South Esk with the 5.11pm from Edinburgh Waverley to Galashiels, 24 May 1962. Photograph W.A.C. Smith.

Type 2 diesel D5310 passing Heriot with the 9.20pm from Carlisle to Edinburgh Waverley on 11 May 1963. Photograph W.A.C. Smith.

B1 4-6-0 61351 tops the 880ft Falahill summit with the 12.05pm from Hawick to Edinburgh Waverley on 11 May 1963. Photograph W.A.C. Smith.

You'll Remember those Black and White Days...

Above. BR Standard 4MT 2-6-0 76049 at Gorebridge with the 12.00pm from Hawick to Edinburgh Waverley on 26 September 1964. Photograph W.A.C. Smith.

Top right. Type 4 Peak diesel D13 with the 2.36pm Edinburgh Waverley to Carlisle, approaching Stow station (the town is seen on the hillside) on 26 May 1962. Photograph Michael Mensing.

Right. BR Standard 2-6-4T 80113 arriving at Galashiels with the 12.5pm Hawick-Edinburgh Waverley on 26 May 1962. Photograph Michael Mensing.

You'll Remember those Black and White Days...

The Feltham Hump

Bryan Wilson

This is the view eastward from the Down Hump Control Cabin on 6 March 1954, just after the first 350hp diesel shunters had arrived. On the extreme left is the Wagon Repair Shop with the Up Marshalling Sidings beyond it. In the centre are ten well-filled Down Reception Roads; an H16 4-6-2T stands on the Engine Line adjacent to the shed. An O2 0-4-4T, probably 30230 (a four-year resident) and a couple of 0395 0-6-0s sit outside the shed. Further over, what looks like a '700' 0-6-0 and a Q1 stand to the left of the coal hopper. We can just see the corrugated cladding on the wagon hoist and tippler of the coaling plant, provided in an effort to keep the dust nuisance to a minimum. Photograph A.R. Carpenter, The Transport Treasury.

In the early years of the twentieth century the London & South Western Railway was, quite frankly, in a pickle so far as its freight services were concerned. Brentford yard received additional sidings in 1906 but could not be extended further. Nevertheless, in 1913 it received six trains daily off the Great Northern and a similar number of trips from Willesden, Brent (Midland) and Neasden. This small yard also managed to despatch direct services to Eastleigh, Reading, Woking and Richmond. The situation was so bad that primary marshalling for LSW destinations was carried out in other company's yards; indeed the South Western maintained a complement of shunters at Brent Midland purely to handle their own traffic.

The new yard at Feltham was the brainchild of the LSW's General Manager (Sir) Herbert Walker. The purchase of 41½ acres of land between Feltham Junction and Feltham station was agreed in July 1910 and more was acquired during the First World War. The first eight sidings (for Down traffic) opened on 9 December 1917. This relieved congestion at Brent and the LSW

shunters there came back home. The new facilities at Feltham were completed for all Down traffic on 3 October 1920 with the Hump Control Cabin coming into use on 2 April 1922. the Down side facilities consisted eventually of ten Reception Roads and twenty Marshalling Sidings.

The new Up Yard came into full use on 2 October 1921. This consisted of eight Reception Roads and sixteen Marshalling Sidings (extended to nineteen about 1938). The whole outfit needed thirty miles of track. No less than 2,500 wagons per day passed through the yard immediately after opening. Subsequently, this figure occasionally rose to nearly 3,400. Some feat for what was considered a 'non-freight' railway!

Because of the shorter length of cross-London trains, services on opening were (Daily):
50 Down Arrivals and 18 Departures
26 Up Arrivals and 46 Departures

Having carried out all this work on the freight side, it made no sense at all to still have the nearest engine shed at Strawberry Hill (a six road shed for thirty locos had been

provided in 1897 and extended in 1907) especially with electrification also eating away at Strawberry Hill's passenger work.

It was decided therefore to build a new shed at Feltham adjacent to the Yard. This was the last engine shed to be built for the LSWR and the first *major* one to be built of concrete for the SR (Okehampton was actually the first). It was a six road 'northlight' shed and came into use in March 1923, men and work transferring in gradually.

Its main claim to fame was that at one time it was 'home' to all the H16 4-6-2 tanks and to all the G16 4-8-0 shunting tanks, not to mention a fleet of eighteen S15 4-6-0s in 1933. The complete engine shed and marshalling yard now took up no less than 79 acres of Hounslow Marsh.

Modernisation and 'rationalisation' took their toll with all the yard sidings taken out of use on 2 March 1969. The shed closed to steam in the spring of 1967 and completely on 9 August 1970. It had been demolished by 1977. A short-lived diesel facility suffered the same fate. Now to Feltham Hump 'at work':

You'll Remember those Black and White Days...

Not very often do we see a brand new 16T mineral wagon but this is one, to diagram 1/108 with no bottom doors, on 6 March 1954. A good view for modellers of the 'non-opening' end. Huts, offices and 'bothies' abound, large and small, corrugated and concrete – and there's always one with a telephone attached. An excellent view of the substantial Wagon Shops. Photograph A.R. Carpenter, The Transport Treasury.

Ex-LMS unfitted goods van 501443, dating from 1934/5 comes over the Hump. For those looking for detail, the door has been renewed with vertical planks at some time, a not-uncommon occurrence. A consignment of rails spread over a match wagon and a couple of single bolsters follow. True 'Southern' materials on the bank! Photograph A.R. Carpenter, The Transport Treasury.

You'll Remember those Black and White Days...

Riley's Railway Roundabout

Northolt Junction(s), 4 May 1957
Notes by Alec Swain

7032 DENBIGH CASTLE approaching South Ruislip with the 10.10am Paddington-Aberystwyth, the 'Cambrian Coast Express' with reporting number '183' on the smokebox door, 4 May 1957. The single line on the right is the Down Line from Marylebone, with connections to both the Down Relief and Down Main lines. The Up Line to Marylebone diverges to the left where the CATCH POINTS sign is. These protected the Up GW/GC junctions. At this point it became the GW&GC Joint Line to Ashendon Junction. Note LT Central Line train to West Ruislip on extreme right. Northolt Junction East Signal Box is just visible to the right of 7032, in the 'V' of the GC and GW tracks. Photograph R.C. Riley, The Transport Treasury.

An unidentified Castle passes South Ruislip station with Cup Final Excursion '084' (no doubt to Paddington as it has the signal OFF for the GW line, not the GC). There were ten football specials that day from the Birmingham area for Wembley, where Aston Villa beat Manchester United 2.1. Mr Riley is standing just off the London end of the Down Platform served by the Down Relief line. Note bridge girder. Photograph R.C. Riley, The Transport Treasury.

You'll Remember those Black and White Days...

2270 (a Banbury engine) approaches Northolt East Junction with a Down freight on the Down Main Line, 4 May 1957. Photograph R.C. Riley, The Transport Treasury.

7918 RHOSE WOOD HALL heads towards London with another Cup Final Excursion that day, '085'. Photograph R.C. Riley, The Transport Treasury.

You'll Remember those Black and White Days...

6014 KING HENRY VII at Northolt East Junction with '353', the 7.30am Shrewsbury-Paddington. South Ruislip Central Line station (island platform) is just visible to the left. The view is from the signal box steps on the Up Main Line. Photograph R.C. Riley, The Transport Treasury.

Wolverhampton Stafford Road Castle 7026 SUDELEY CASTLE heads for London with another Up Special train '087' passing Northolt Jc. East signal box (note 'Jc.' on name board). Photograph R.C. Riley, The Transport Treasury.

7032 DENBIGH CASTLE (see the first picture) comes back south, heading for Paddington with '183' (again!), the Up Cambrian Coast Express. Note the Up GC single line on the right and the Down GC single line on the left. Presumably 7032 would have worked to Wolverhampton, turned and worked back. It was a long day for the photographer... Photograph R.C. Riley, The Transport Treasury.

4988 BULWELL HALL, a lined black Tyseley Hall, on the Down GC single line approaching Northolt East Junction with a return excursion '088' from Wembley Hill. Photograph R.C. Riley, The Transport Treasury.

4092 DUNRAVEN CASTLE approaching Northolt East Junction with '196' down from Paddington. The Up single line to GC on the left, Down line from GC just visible on the right. Note the Down Relief line starts here and continues through to West Ruislip. Photograph R.C. Riley, The Transport Treasury.

6020 KING HENRY IV with '195', the 6.10pm Paddington-Birkenhead, approaches Northolt East Junction signalled through on the Down Main. This is where the Up Relief and Down Relief lines diverged/joined. There is an A3 Pacific on that single line Down GC connection, showing how it 'burrowed' beneath the GW line! In a remarkable display of enginemanship, the Pacific ground its way at walking pace along the curve, allowing the WR train to clear the line; the ER train then joined the main line without stopping. Note disused spectacle (no arm) on signal post (lenses removed!). Photograph R.C. Riley, The Transport Treasury.

FROM NORBURY TO NORTHAM

There was hardly a station in south London that did not see at least the odd incendiary, or a sprinkling of shrapnel as the German bombing intensified from the autumn of 1940. Norbury station (top) was one of a number badly knocked about during that time; this was the dazed scene at 11.30am on 29 October 1940. Out in the countryside of Kent, Surrey and Sussex matters were easier but in some coastal towns, especially those with a strategic element, such as Dover, Portsmouth and Plymouth, experiences were harsh indeed. And then of course, there was Southampton; of the great port the official Southern Railway account says: 'If ever a place was predestined to air attack this was it'. And so it was – this is Northam station on the edge of the city on 2 December 1940, after two days described as 'really dreadful'. In the restrained tones of the time this meant things were as awful as they get. The freezing cold made everything worse. Workers were soon being evacuated and a few days later the King paid an encouraging visit.

You'll Remember those Black and White Days...

Late Glories on the GN
Notes by Peter Coster

Class A2/3 60523 SUN CASTLE heads a Leeds and Bradford express past the site of Tunnel signalbox on 18 August 1962. A two car DMU has surmounted the steep climb from Wood Green (now Alexandra Palace) to the flyover for the New Line to Hertford. On the right is the down goods from the 'Khyber Pass' seen in the distance, into which come the sidings from beneath the flyover and, on the extreme right, from the Brickfields Sidings. The latter was the site of a brickworks which, I believe, contributed to the construction of Wood Green Tunnel. Photograph Peter Groom.

Class A3 60061 PRETTY POLLY heads the 17.05 north of Finsbury Park during the last week of steam south of Peterborough. Although nearly forty years old, the unfortunately-named veteran is beautifully clean and the haze from the chimney hardly gives any impression of the effort required to get her heavy train up to speed. The photographer is standing on down slow two, and the wooden pegs show that even this track has its alignment designed and defined. It was such attention to detail that made Kings Cross District track a byword for perfection. Photograph Peter Groom.

Class A4 60017 SILVER FOX in absolutely immaculate condition heads the 16.30 'Parley' to Peterborough out of Wood Green Tunnel. One has to look at the lamp positions to see that it is a class 'B', and to realise that it is not in fact a far more prestigious duty! Photograph Peter Groom.

Class A4 No.60007 SIR NIGEL GRESLEY, now preserved, heads the 'Talisman' north of Finsbury Park on 14 June 1962. Again the engine is working hard but there is a fairly clean exhaust. Notice also that the eight coach train has grown to ten; in the next week Deltics took over on new comprehensive diagrams. Photograph Peter Groom.

You'll Remember those Black and White Days...

In the same location Class A3 60056 CENTENARY heads the 17.00 down from Kings Cross, 14 June 1962. Again the train has lengthened from the usual eight cars of the early 1950s, to eleven. Photograph Peter Groom.

One of the first batch of 9F 2-10-0s at New England, 92044 heads an up mineral past the Pullman Car Company's siding north of Finsbury Park, 30 May 1960. Quite where it was going I cannot explain, because the only options were East Goods Yard and Kings Cross Goods Yard, neither of which dealt with coal so far as I can remember. The most probable explanation is that it was bound for East Goods where it would be broken up and rakes distributed to yards in north London. Photograph Peter Groom.

SILVER FOX, again in immaculate condition, heads the 16.05 Kings Cross to York north of Finsbury Park on 31 May 1962. The driver has seen Haringay's distant off, showing that the 'Talisman' has got clear, and opened the regulator. Photograph Peter Groom.

An unusual view north of Hatfield on 14 May 1959 and Class A2/3 60520 OWEN TUDOR heads a down evening 'Parley' north. The two tracks nearest the camera are the Dunstable single line and the down slow. On the far side of the two main lines are the up slow, and the Hertford single line via Cole Green. A 'Swedey', N7 0-6-2T, heads a down Dunstable or empty stock on the Dunstable single line. Photograph Peter Groom.

You'll Remember those Black and White Days...

Kings and Castles at Exeter
Notes by E.S. Youldon

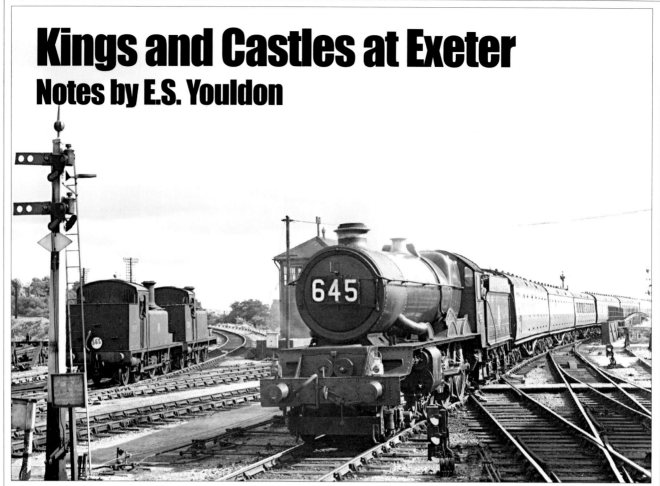

King 4-6-0 6023 KING EDWARD II approaches with the 11.50am Penzance to Paddington on 7 August 1954 while bankers E1R 0-6-2Ts 32135 and 32124 descend from Exeter Central. The notice in the foreground informs us that the bell will ring when engines or vehicles are approaching from Exeter Central or from South Devon sidings. Photograph J. Robertson, The Transport Treasury.

6025 KING HENRY III in charge of the 8.30am Plymouth to Paddington on Saturday 6 August 1955. The fireman is shovelling coal forward to ease the task later on. Photograph J. Robertson, The Transport Treasury.

Castle 4-6-0 5006 TREGENNA CASTLE (which later was really an hotel!) takes the down through road hauling the 10.40am Paddington-Paignton on Saturday 6 August 1955. The distinctive Middle Box is prominent. Photograph J. Robertson, The Transport Treasury.

Kings in and out on 6 August 1955. 6017 KING EDWARD IV runs through with the down Cornish Riviera while another King forges away towards Cowley Bridge. Photograph J. Robertson, The Transport Treasury.

You'll Remember those Black and White Days...

KING EDWARD V now graces the station, on 17 August 1957 with the 8.50am Paddington-Paignton service. 6016 sports the new front end it received in 1954 – the strengthened lifting holes at the front being the give-away. Fourteen Kings were given this treatment over the years from 1954 to 1958. A Bulleid Pacific just gets into the picture on the left. Photograph J. Robertson, The Transport Treasury.

Something a bit out of the ordinary to end up with – bullnosed 5005 MANORBIER CASTLE departs from Platform 6 and over Red Cow crossing with an up express in the late 1930s. This Castle was semi-streamlined in March 1935 but while some of the sections were removed the following September other features, including the 'bullnose', remained until June 1943. Note the casual regard for personal safety and apparent lack of concern from the crossing keeper – the gent below the large notice! Photograph The Transport Treasury.
Particular thanks to Derek Frost in the compilation of these notes.

Diesel Dawn
Here and There

Of all the bewildering variety of diesel power that began arriving on BR from the late 1950s perhaps the oddest-looking were the North British Type 2s, both the diesel-electric and diesel-hydraulic versions. They were designed from the first to be used frequently in pairs so the need to have gangway doors is some consolation at least for the peculiar 'cut-off' look at the ends. They were also notable for the use of spoked wheels... Neither of course was a success, though the diesel-electric D6100s were probably the poorer of the two types. D6108 and D6105 (top) are at New England shed on the ER on 10 April 1960, and would be on their way to Glasgow for repairs (or on their way back). At least the lower pair, D6331 and D6321, will be actually working. They are standing in the yard at Swindon on 16 October 1960. Photographs Frank Hornby.

You'll Remember those Black and White Days...

Although all sort of permutations were possible, the track layout through Barking encompassed three main routings: BR steam trains Fenchurch Street to Shoeburyness or Tilbury, BR steam freight from the Midland Division via Kentish Town towards Tilbury serving North Thameside, and London Transport Underground services on the District line via central London to Upminster. Although the BR LTS section suburban services and the LT services basically kept to their own double tracks through Barking the heavy freight flow needed to cross both of these other routes and did so over a complex set of diamond crossings at Barking East Junction. There were over 700 movements across this area of trackwork each day with innumerable conflicting movements. These problems had been greatly exacerbated by the extension of District line trains to Upminster on 12th September 1932. It presented a major operational difficulty that was gradually getting worse as the post-war years saw increased industrial traffic along the north shore of the lower Thames. There was also a need to augment the District line frequency as South East Essex grew after the war.

This situation was understandably deemed intolerable in the light of the electrification plans for the LTS suburban service and a radical rebuilding of the whole Barking area was conceived. This stretched from a new BR EMU depot that was to be built on the site of Little Ilford Up Sidings and the old LT electric stock sidings at the same location – a mile west of Barking – through to a new hump yard to serve North Thameside at Ripple Lane east of Barking. The plans included an additional double track bridge over the River Roding, two new flyovers west of Barking station to segregate traffic previously getting in each other's way at East

East Street road bridge over the east end of Barking station, looking north-eastwards on 20 March 1956. The station buildings opened in December 1907 and with the associated road bridge, which replaced a notorious level crossing, were part of the 1906-1908 rebuilding when the LTSR was quadrupled from East Ham to Barking. Demolished and replaced by temporary facilities for the duration of the rebuilding scheme, it was ultimately succeeded by impressive new premises that opened 29 September 1959. A London Transport RT family bus pulls into the road in the distance whilst the trolleybus wires supply power for routes 691 and 693 which were only to survive until 18 August 1959. Public transport in Barking was being totally transformed.

All Change At Barking

By Alan Godsave

You'll Remember those Black and White Days...

Junction, recasting the platform usage through the four island platforms at Barking and a new dive-under for westbound LT trains east of the station. Also part of the improvements was new station building on a widened East Street road bridge.

The aims were to eliminate the conflicts across flat junctions, totally segregate London Transport and B.R. tracks, signalling etc, introduce cross-platform interchange between BR LTS and LT Underground services in both directions at Barking station, find a location for the depot needed to maintain the LTS fleet of EMUs and close five smaller yards – Plaistow Up and Down, the existing Ripple Lane Up and Down and Little Ilford yard. Unlike major works today, this was all implemented without serious disruption to the very busy LTS and LT traffic although at weekends LTS steam services could be found on the Underground lines. Work started in July 1956 and continued through many, many stages until the new station was officially opened on 29th September 1961, well before the last LTS steam service from Fenchurch Street on 18th June 1962. Multi-aspect colour lights superseded life expired semaphores and the whole area lost its manual signal boxes to be replaced by a new power interlocking at Barking.

Above. On 20 March 1956, with Barking East signal box to the left, the photographer is standing on the double tracks linking platforms 2 and 3 at Barking station (principally served by trains to and from the Midland at Kentish Town) and – behind his back – the original LTS route to Tilbury. This was the route of the majority of the freight traffic and there were these six fixed diamond crossings where it crossed the up LTS main line from Southend and Upminster to Fenchurch Street. Its down equivalent is beyond and the westbound LT line from Upminster towards the City is furthest away with a westbound District train having just rattled across. All in all, this area of trackwork – showing signs of poor alignment caused by very heavy use – carried over 700 trains each 24 hours. The replacement of this series of flat crossings was the main driving force behind the series of flyovers and dive-unders that were to transform the Barking area in the late 1950s.

Below. Looking east under Queen's Road bridge as Fairburn 2-6-4T 42684 leaves on an up ECS train, 9 September 1953. The photographer is standing between the up and down running lines used by LT District and Hammersmith & City services whose colour light signals stand out amongst the BR semaphores. BR steam trains did use these lines but the main traffic to Fenchurch Street used the pair on the right and the services via the Tottenham & Forest Gate Joint and the Tottenham and Hampstead Joint to Kentish Town and St Pancras used the pair on the left. The MR arms on the LTS bracket to the right include the down splitting distants for Barking East. An LTS ground signal nestles at the foot of the post.

A lovely west end panorama from the footbridge, 20 March 1956. A departing London-bound LT district line train leaves platform 5 and passes Barking West signal box. Platforms 1, 2, 3, 4 and 5 were electrified for LT use although No.1 only had occasional use and platform 4 was for terminating trains only as the track did not extend much beyond the far end of the platform. Beyond Queen's Road bridge the high down home signal and splitting distant are set for a down Southend direction LTS steam working, while on the vast expanses of platform gas lights outnumber passengers.

Eastward towards the London end of the islands that form platforms 1/2, 3/4 and 5/6 from left to right, 20 April 1956. Platform 4 – behind the LT colour light signal – was a dead end solely used by terminating LT trains. Again the scarcity of trains and passengers is noticeable. The basic platform formation survived the major work connected with the LTS electrification but the uses to which the various platform faces were put in 1956 were soon to be fundamentally changed.

Looking towards Tilbury and Southend we see an almost deserted Barking station, in the form that resulted from the 1906-08 rebuilding. It consisted of four 700 feet long island platforms with numbers 1 and 2 nearest the camera beyond the two down loops. The symmetry of the buildings and canopies on the islands is pleasing but the piecemeal construction of the footbridge spoils the effect. The date is 20 April 1956. The newer addition to the footbridge on the north side dated from the late 1940s.

A goodly crowd of passengers await a down LTS train towards Southend or Tilbury on platform 6, 20 April 1956. They have probably changed platforms having alighted from an eastbound LT service – a major activity at Barking. The photographer is under the footbridge at the west end of the platforms looking south-east with East Street bridge and Barking East signal box beyond. They would have to wait until June 1962 for their onward service in another electric train.

A fascinating photograph looking westwards with Tanners Road footbridge framing an approaching eastbound LT District line train led by what appears to be a Q27 motor coach, 9 September 1953. The route is set across the double junction from the LT lines to the Kentish Town lines with the signal cleared for the entry to platform 2 – the usual pattern for the eastbound District service. The splitting distant signals on the gantry belong to Barking East and control the split that leads to the flat crossing east of the station. The Fenchurch Street steam lines lie on the far left of this view with the down goods loop to the right.

You'll Remember those Black and White Days...

With platform 1 over on the left this shot shows the temporary platform for terminating trains from Kentish Town that was built whilst the major rebuilding works were underway – converted out of the more northerly of the previous down goods loops. A three coach service to Kentish Town or St. Pancras awaits departure on 18 September 1958.

The London end of platforms 1 and 2, on 9 September 1953. The electrified double track leading from platforms 2 and 3 is the route to the Tottenham and Forest Gate Joint and the Tottenham and Hampstead Joint and towards the Midland division at Kentish Town. The LT four rail electrification through these platforms was added to the 1908 scheme in 1911 and allowed increased flexibility of working. City-bound Underground trains would take the connection to the left to reach their double track route towards East Ham. Note amongst the lovely period clutter the LT fog repeater signal added to the lattice post of the LMS starter on platform 3 and Barking West box with Queen's Road bridge beyond. It signalled both BR and LT trains and also dated from the 1908 LTSR quadrupling to Barking; the box opened on 23 February of that year.

Our intrepid photographer is now beyond the London end of the platform 7 and 8 island and standing on the up goods loop, on 20 April 1956. An unidentified BR Standard 2-6-4T is ready to depart from platform 7 with a Fenchurch Street 'stopper' while in the up loop stands 42503, one of the LTS section's Stanier three cylinder 2-6-4Ts awaiting the road with up ECS. Barking West signal box is just out of the picture to the left.

The footbridge at the London end of the station frames this photograph featuring the LT electrified tracks through platforms 4 and 5, 20 April 1956. A city-bound service stands in platform 5 with a terminated train beyond platform 4. Note the LT mechanical device in the foreground that causes a full brake application by raising the arm at track level to operate a brake valve on the train when the signal beyond is at danger – the so-called trip-cock. A train of empty coaching stock stands in the up loop beyond platform 8.

During the period that the various changes at Barking were being managed on a staged basis, two LTS section steam workings stand in platforms 4 and 5, on 16 June 1959. Previously platform 5 formed the main westbound LT platform and platform 4 was solely used by terminating LT trains. Now we see the bunker of a Stanier three cylinder 2-6-4T waiting with a down stopping service and the rear of a Fenchurch Street bound train on its left; they stand on new flat-bottomed non-electrified track.

The new concrete footbridge built as part of the grand Barking scheme to span four tracks at the Ripple Road level crossing just on the Tilbury side of the East Junction at Barking. This was the point where the up and down goods loops extending eastwards from Barking East Junction merged with the main Tilbury-bound double track. The new footbridge was built to span four tracks as construction of the new hump yard at Ripple Lane would see these loops extended to the new yard. But the track usage would be transformed with the old freight loops extended and upgraded to form the up and down Tilbury through lines around the perimeter of the yard while the erstwhile passenger lines would become the up and down freight lines serving the yard. Rippleside signal box stood here until the new Barking interlocking took over its functions.

You'll Remember those Black and White Days...

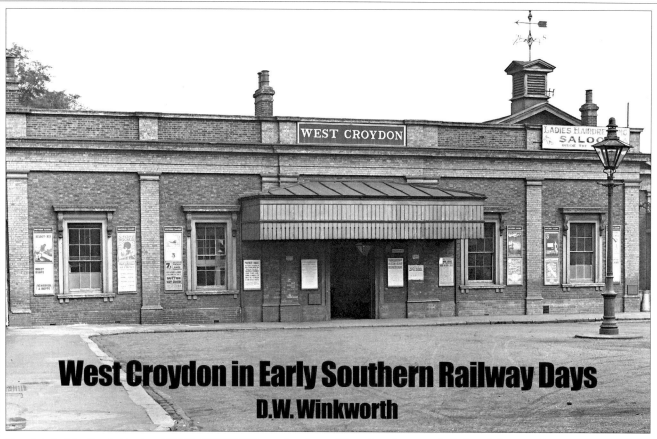

West Croydon in Early Southern Railway Days
D.W. Winkworth

Unmistakably the lettering WEST CROYDON marks the station building as of London, Brighton and South Coast Railway origin. A year has passed since the railway amalgamation of 1923 and the billboards reflect this with the SOUTHERN RAILWAY heading. The site was the Croydon Canal's basin bought by the railway which opened to Croydon in 1839 and the building (top left) was at right angles to the running lines. The station approach from London Road was horseshoe-on-plan with northern and southern gateways. It served as the up side building (there was one for the down side in Station Road) until the early 1930s when the SR rebuilt the station with a new building right up to the London Road building line.

The view bottom left is of the northern access to the station from London Road, where Mr Goodsell's fruiterer and greengrocery business flourished at no.2. The sturdy three-storey building at first served as offices for the London & Croydon Railway and later on became the stationmaster's house, although the bedraggled curtains in the picture suggests it was no longer occupied by January 1924 when these pictures were taken. In the background is part of the station façade while the tall post on the right looks like a tram standard (numbered 25 or, more likely, 125) complete with bamboo pole for turning the trolley boom of the tramcars. The second view (top right) of this building is toward the northern access to London Road. Part of the eaves appears to have become detached. Sainsbury's shop at nos.9 and 11 London Road still stands, despite change of use, long after the railway buildings had been demolished and rejoices in being a public house with the engaging name Ship Of Fools. The first bridge (lower right) over the railway after leaving West Croydon for London was St James' Road known locally (at first) as 'brick bridge' and then later 'Spurgeons' Bridge' taking the name of the Baptist Chapel ('Spurgeons' Tabernacle') built on the west side of the bridge by the brothers Spurgeon. This view is towards West Croydon and features the overhead equipment for the AC electrification

favoured by the LB&SC; it had a short working life (1 April 1925 to 21 September 1929). An odd incident occurred on 10 February 1927 when the station foreman at Selhurst noticed that the quarter light of a third class compartment of the 6.30pm Sutton to London Victoria train, in which two ladies were seated, was broken. The passengers were requested to change into another compartment, the damaged one locked and the guard informed of the circumstances. Upon arrival at Victoria the damaged compartment was examined and a trolley head was found having become detached from a Croydon Corporation tram car when passing over the bridge and projected into the train passing below. The passengers had made no complaint; whether they had joined the train at Selhurst or, somewhat unlikely, were occupying the compartment, was not clear. The question of recovering the cost of repairs to the compartment from the Croydon Corporation was set in motion.

You'll Remember those Black and White Days...

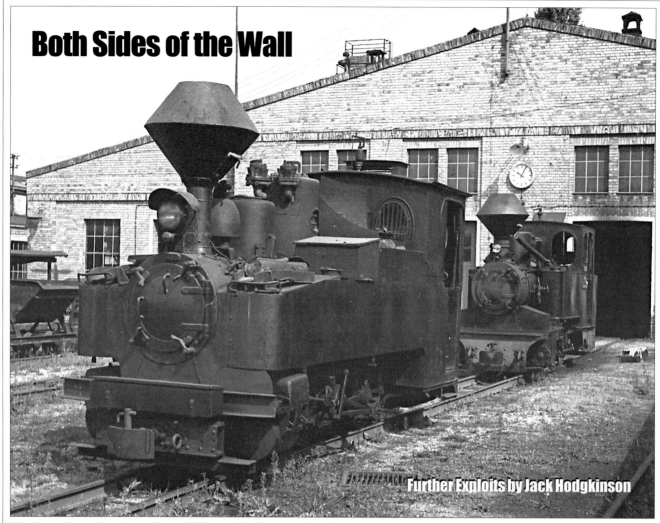

Both Sides of the Wall

Further Exploits by Jack Hodgkinson

The East. Deutsche Reichsbahn (DR) Bad Muskau shed and workshops on the 600mm narrow gauge lines right on the border with Poland near Cottbus, 26 August 1970. The locos are World War One 'Heeresfeldbahn' 0-8-0Ts, 99.3314 and, behind, 99.3312. Six locos were observed there, including two undergoing general overhauls. It was an extensive network, operating a freight only service to various paper mills and so on. Footplate rides were arranged on the spot and our feisty lady guide took a turn on one, showing the all-male company she wasn't afraid of getting her hands dirty! Photograph Jack Hodgkinson.

Early in 1968 with the 'writing on the wall' for steam power on BR, I was working in the Regional Control Room (Eastern Region South) at Hamilton House, Bishopsgate, London. The 'Hamilton' referred to was none other then 'Claud Hamilton' of D16 renown, and one of the engine's nameplates was exhibited on the walls in the reception area. When the time came for us to merge with York HQ and move there, Hamilton House was still populated by Liverpool Street District Control and I hoped 'Claud' would be left in safe hands. Before the merger took place I was persuaded by two younger members of staff (both keen enthusiasts and photographers) to join them on a weekend visit to depots around the Ruhr and the line between Osnabruck and Bremen. This visit was highly successful and encouraged me to make other incursions into *Das Vaterland* especially around the Rheine-Emden line which was very busy with both freight and passenger traffic, and also nicely placed for the Dutch

frontier and connections with the ferry over from Harwich to Hook of Holland. My non-existent German now included such phrases as 'Do you have a single room for the night, with breakfast?'

Speaking of catching the ferry, we had made advanced plans to sail on it on one occasion when a rail strike intervened. It was Eastern Region policy to duplicate boat services at all costs by road transport and this had made the BBC1 nine o'clock television news with footage of yours truly stepping on board the motor coach at Liverpool Street immediately behind a rather good looking fur-coated lady. Several 'friends' rang my wife to tell her the glad tidings about my assumed infidelity!

For added spice, the Osnabruck visit also included a brief foray to Helmstedt – then the frontier between West Germany and the notorious East. Our prime object was to see an international West-East express re-engined with a candidate from the *Deutsche Reichsbahn* from the other side of the

'Iron Curtain'. This was duly accomplished and we were just hanging about taking a photographic interest in an old Prussian 2-8-0 stationary boiler when the *Polizei* descended and insisted we took the next train back to Brauschweig – which was our intention anyway.

Seeing my first DR loco was an inspiration, and I wanted more. 'Gricing' was strictly *verboten* under communism; all movements were regarded as 'strategic' and official displeasure concerning photography also extended to station and depot architecture.

The only sure way of getting a successful visit with photographic records was to go with an enthusiast organisation – which prompted me to join the LCGB and accompany them in 1970. Our entry into the GDR was via overnight train to Magdeburg and our slumbers were rudely interrupted at some unearthly hour in Oebisfelde, the East German frontier station. We were all ordered from a train and herded into some cold damp waiting room while the 'goon-squad' with

You'll Remember those Black and White Days...

their four-legged Alsatian friends went over the train from top to bottom. The search would be fruitless so far we were concerned but this was communist customer care at its best.

Following a microscopic scrutiny of passports and the all-important visas, we were allowed back on board. Oebisfelde really was a one-horse town and I see it has lost its prestigious inclusion in Thomas Cook's European Timetable nowadays.

The tour included Berlin, its western flank, Cottbus on the Polish border and the far south to Aue and Saalfeld. At Berlin Lichtenburg depot tables were laid out with an array of hardware such as smokebox numberplates and cabside adornments, all on sale for Western currency. Though reasonable to us this represented a small fortune to our hosts compared with their worthless Reichsmarks. Our assigned guide was a lady who soon cottoned on to our requirements and she was to be congratulated on her achievements within the ultra-sensitive authoritarian presence. This was reflected in her report back to her superiors at the end of the tour, but in the column devoted to 'political success' she had to record a big fat zero. A little souvenir line for which she was instrumental in acting as go-between involved some superb scale models of the Prussian G10 tender loco with a gilt finish. These were to be had from the chef in some hotel restaurant under cover of napkins, with the western currency channelled back to the kitchen covered by slices of bread and out of the sight of 'big brother'.

The only hitch occurred one morning at breakfast when a head count revealed one member missing. No one knew his whereabouts (or they weren't saying) and it was not until dinner that evening when he turned up. Apparently on the previous trip our 'missing' friend had made the acquaintance of a young *fraulein* and this was the perfect way for them to be reunited – if only for a day. His reappearance obviously was a big relief for the party leader for it could have had serious repercussions for the Club. My last visit to the GDR was in 1980 when I accompanied some West German friends (from Hof) to Saalfeld. Going in was OK and I had to book the compulsory room for one night at the *'Goldener Adler'* although I had no intention of staying. The price was cheap for the expectation of clandestine camera activity, which we accomplished, but getting out was somewhat trickier. My friend was a Mercedes salesman and we were making use of his 'office perk' for transport. This vehicle made border guards take a more then usual interest and they went over (and under) it with a fine tooth comb. My salesman friend's pockets revealed scores of bits of paper with telephone numbers on – which he was grilled over at length. Then they found some sets of transparencies in the dash (they had been bought earlier on at the DB rail museum in Neunmarkt-Wirsburg) and these really inflamed the situation. When it came to my turn, they gave my loaned Zenit (Russian) SLR the once-over and deliberately opened the back to fog the film. After we were handed our passports back my hosts were deeply ashamed at the behaviour of their fellow countrymen – but that was life only a couple of decades or so ago, back in 1980. I never expected to see a reunified Germany in my lifetime but it happened; I still have those fogged pictures to remind me of the bad old days.

Deutsche Reichsbahn (DR) 39 class 2-8-2 39.1061.9 departs Saalfeld on 28 August 1970. These elegant three cylinder locos were built as class P10 from 1922 onwards for the Prussian State Railways and were rebuilt between 1958 and 1962 from their Belpaire firebox form, getting standard boilers and new tenders. Photograph Jack Hodgkinson.

You'll Remember those Black and White Days...

Deutsche Reichsbahn (DR) Saxon Meyer four cylinder 0-4-4-0T 99.1606.5 ready to take to the streets of Wilkau-Haslau on 27 August 1970 on the 750mm line to Kirchberg. This was about five miles long and ran by the roadside, and was heavily graded – Kirchberg shed had al allocation of four of these Meyers with two in steam daily. Photograph Jack Hodgkinson.

Deutsche Reichsbahn (DR) Prussian G8.2 2-8-0 56.2009 (a class built 1919-1927 and now equipped with cab radio – the antenna protrudes from the cab roof) in the yards at Goschwitz, 28 August 1970. The author of the club 'Bulletin' later remarked : 'it was a surprise to find a Cl.56 in steam and an almost unique opportunity to see one as a yard pilot'. Photograph Jack Hodgkinson.

Deutsche Reichsbahn (DR) Class 62 1007-4, one of fifteen 4-6-4Ts built 1928-29, at Berlin Lichtenburg shed on 25 August 1970. One of the class, 62-1015, survived into preservation and had the honour of hauling the first leg out of Berlin to the Polish border with the British-organised 'excursion' entirely steam hauled to Vladivostok – at enormous expense! Photograph Jack Hodgkinson.

A Deutsche Reichsbahn (DR) Prussian G8.1 type 0-8-0 dating from World War One, 55.4602 at Berlin Lichtenburg, 25 August 1970. Lichtenburg was little more than an island platform but it handled plenty of traffic with its own 'rush hour'. The G8-1 could have been in use for stock disposal/procurement. Photograph Jack Hodgkinson.

You'll Remember those Black and White Days...

A Deutsche Bundesbahn (DB) 2-10-0 with cabin-tender, 051.7581 brings passengers off the Friesian Islands ferry at Emden Docks up to the Hbf, 20 August 1970. ('Hbf.' is the standard German abbreviation for 'Hauptbahnhof – i.e. Central or Main Station.) Photograph Jack Hodgkinson.

Deutsche Bundesbahn (DB) Oil burning Pacific 01.1076 waits time at Bremen with a Hamburg express, 29 March 1968. They were built before the war but were very capable performers over this route. Photograph Jack Hodgkinson.

Deutsche Reichsbahn (DR) 2-8-2 41.225 backs down from the 'Iron Curtain' at Helmstedt to re-engine the Hook of Holland-Berlin express, 31 March 1968. The (armed) great-coated figure taking a keen interest in me is there to ensure the crew do not make a bid for freedom. 'Glasnost' was still a long way off and though GDR citizens might enjoy a few hours in the 'West' absconding was not an option. Our guide was a Berliner who could visit West Berlin on occasion but NEVER with her husband or as a family. Photograph Jack Hodgkinson.

Deutsche Bundesbahn (DB) Class 44 2-10-0 44.1680 in good company at Braunschweig shed, 30 March 1968. Some of these German classes certainly seemed to exude an aura of power. Photograph Jack Hodgkinson.

You'll Remember those Black and White Days...

Deutsche Reichsbahn (DR) Prussian T16 0-10-0T 094-361-3 rejoins the main line at Emden Yard for more wagon-load dock traffic from the exchange sidings, 20 August 1970. Block loads of imported ore originated from the docks and would bypass the exchange sidings. Photograph Jack Hodgkinson.

Diesel Dawn
When They Used to Clean Them

For a period the new diesels, Warships most notably, gleamed and shone just as the brass sparkled and the green livery shimmered on the steam locomotives alongside. For one brought up in rather humbler climes, the effect at Paddington in 1960 was mesmerising. Here are two typical Warships of the time, at Old Oak Common before the venerable system of roundhouses was transformed into a diesel depot. Top is D834 PATHFINDER on one of the 'Factory' roads (note the tender behind) in August 1960; relatively free of smoke and dust, this was the best place to maintain the first diesel arrivals. Below is D859 VANQUISHER (electrification flashes and yellow end panels have arrived in the meantime) in January 1962. Alongside is the old 1947 oil fuel plant adapted for diesel fuelling – the water column-like apparatus beyond is one of the old fuel oil 'columns' to fit steam locomotive tenders. Photographs A.F. Cottrell, The Transport Treasury.

You'll Remember those Black and White Days...

THE CALEY
Keith Miles

56025

BRITISH R

During my time in Glasgow if asked where I worked I would reply, as would have any of my workmates, 'Up at the Caley'. To Glaswegians this could only mean one place, St Rollox, the former Caledonian Railway's Locomotive & Carriage Works on the heights of Springburn. Despite ownership having passed to the LMS over two decades earlier, the name had still stuck and I should be interested to learn how long it continued to do so through the vicissitudes of modernisation, rationalisation, privatisation and the various other gratuitous metamorphoses visited upon the railways. Meantime, let's go back to the very beginning.

The city's first steam railway was the 4ft 6in gauge Garnkirk & Glasgow opened in 1831, a predominantly mineral line from the Monklands coalfield which terminated at Townhead, just west of Springburn Road. In due course the railway became the Glasgow, Garnkirk & Coatbridge in 1844 and was taken over by the Caledonian in 1847 who relaid it to standard gauge. On completion of the company's main line from the south in 1848 Townhead briefly became the city's first terminus for Anglo-Scottish traffic, until the opening of Buchanan Street in 1849. Before these later developments, however, the Garnkirk & Glasgow had by 1835 built its own small locomotive, carriage and wagon works on the east side of Springburn Road adjacent to what was then Inchbelly level crossing.

By the early 1850s the Caledonian's former Glasgow, Paisley & Greenock works at the latter place was becoming overwhelmed by the demands of the bigger company and a decision was taken to move most operations to Glasgow by enlarging the G&G works. The new St Rollox works was opened in 1856, the old works becoming the boiler shop, with 350 workers transferred from Greenock. On a domestic note, the company

The works 'Pug' simmers outside the Erecting Shop in August 1948 soon after acquiring its first BR identity following a service repair occasioned by a burst boiler tube. At subsequent works visits it was given full passenger livery, even to the extent of lining the cab front. Built during the Drummond era as CR No.515 in May 1890, it came to St Rollox from Dawsholm in 1939 in replacement for 16005 which had had the job since 1925. However, it retained its 27K shedplate until going through the works in January 1947 when the plate was removed and came into my possession. 56025 was withdrawn in May 1960 after seventy years service. Photograph Rex Conway Steam Railway Collection.

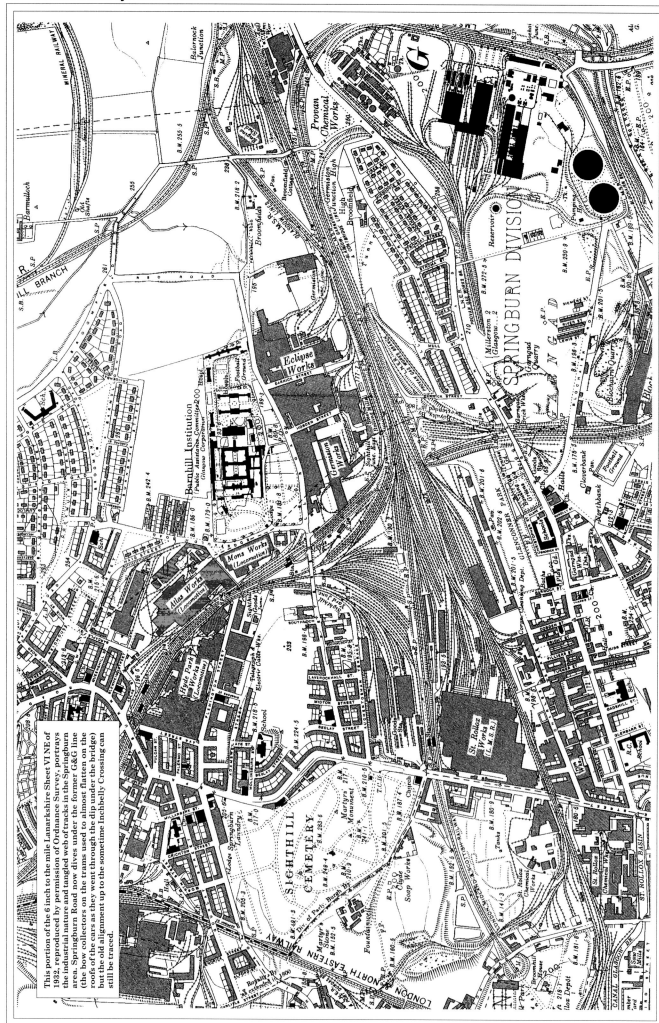

This portion of the 6 inch to the mile Lanarkshire Sheet VI NE of 1932, reproduced by permission of Ordnance Survey, portrays the industrial nature and tangled web of tracks in the Springburn area. Springburn Road now dives under the former G&G line (the bow collectors on the trams used to almost flatten on the roofs of the cars as they went through the dip under the bridge) but the old alignment up to the sometime Inchbelly Crossing can still be traced.

Caledonian days and a proud crew pose with McIntosh 900 class or Dunalastair III 4-4-0 897 built at St Rollox in 1900. Pickersgill rebuilt four of the class with superheated boilers but 897 only received a new saturated boiler in 1919. However, in 1930, as 14347, it was given the superheated boiler off the withdrawn 900, new cylinders, piston valves and a six-wheeled tender. It was withdrawn in March 1939 and the last of the class in service was 14338 withdrawn in March 1946. It was outlived, nonetheless, by 14348 which, although withdrawn in August 1944, soldiered on as a stationary boiler at Kilmarnock Works until at least the Autumn of 1947. Photograph: Keith Miles Collection.

agreed to issue these men with passes in order to seek out accommodation in Springburn and, in due course, transported them, their families, goods and chattels to St Rollox. From here the men arranged and paid for their final move to new homes round about.

Contemporaneously, the one-time village of Springburn Cross had developed rapidly as an industrial centre with a high proportion of immigrant workers, including many from the Scottish Highlands or Ireland. Even as late as 1914 the Springburn Wards had the highest proportion of Irish born in Glasgow. From a railway point of view, the Edinburgh & Glasgow had arrived in 1840 in the shape of some 15,000 navvies which led to the opening of the line down to Queen Street in 1842. The company built their works at the top of the incline on the other side of Sighthill Cemetery from St Rollox and named it after the nearby Cowlairs estate.

Nearby, extraordinarily, two other locomotive works were established before the end of the century. In 1862 Walter Montgomerie Neilson moved his business from Finnieston into the new Hyde Park Works, named after the street where his Clydeside factory had been sited. The following year his manager, Henry Dubs, left and formed the Glasgow Locomotive Co at Queen's Park. Furthermore, in 1872, amid some acrimony, James Reid bought out Neilson whilst retaining the name. Walter departed abroad in high dudgeon but returned in 1884 to set up the Clyde Locomotive Works cheek by jowl with his rival. Not surprisingly, perhaps, business was poor and in 1888 he succumbed to an offer by Sharp Stewart to move their Atlas Works operation from Manchester. In 1903 all three, Hyde Park, Atlas and Queen's Park Works, amalgamated to form the North British Locomotive Co, a name to be conjured with throughout the Empire and beyond.

These enterprises were rail connected, of course, as were the other concerns in the area – the malodorous Tennants Chemical Works whose proprietors had been the chief sponsors of the G&G, Braby's Eclipse galvanised iron works, Provan Gas Works, Blochairn Iron Works, to name but a few. Together with the burgeoning railway system, including its various sidings and yards, the area soon became a concentrated web of tracks, as illustrated by the accompanying map. But back to St Rollox...

A new wagon shop and paint shop had been added in 1868 but little had changed so far as locomotive matters were concerned. By 1882 the capabilities of the company's engine fleet were falling short of requirements and the workshop facilities were unable to cope with the increased workload. Furthermore, the Locomotive Superintendent, George Brittain, was in poor health. Over at Cowlairs sweeping changes had been made by a forceful young man they'd recruited from Brighton so the Caledonian directors, grasping the nettle, invited 42 year old Dugald Drummond to take charge at St Rollox at twice his predecessor's salary. His resultant improvements in the locomotive stock are well documented and probably outside the scope of this story but few can be unaware of his 0-6-0 Standard Goods or 'Jumbos' as they came to be known. Perpetuated by his successors, a total of 244 were built up to 1897 and all but half a dozen passed into British Railways, the last being withdrawn as late as 1963 after nearly eighty years service.

On his arrival Drummond found that some repairs were still being carried out at Greenock and also at Perth, the former Scottish Central Railway works. He determined to concentrate all major work, both repairs and new construction of locomotives, carriages and wagons at St Rollox and initiated a massive reorganisation. Remarkably, this was accomplished by 1885 and the new buildings, some three times the size of the originals, extended from the former G&G tracks to the line down to Buchanan Street, all under one continuous roof. The upheaval,

LMS days and 14497 stands in the works yard finished in the post-1928 red-lined black livery with red-shaded gold letters and numerals. Unusually it still retains its smokebox numberplate. As CR No.66 it was the first of a dozen 72 class engines built at NBL's Hyde Park Works in 1922. Both classes of Pickersgill 4-4-0s were easily distinguished from their McIntosh predecessors by the long, wide, separate splasher over the connecting rods. One of them, 14463, proved to be the last pre-grouping 4-4-0 to survive on BR; it was withdrawn in December 1962 but remained in store at Carstairs until November 1964. Photograph: James Stevenson.

of course, jeopardised production and thirty-five Jumbos and ten class 66 4-4-0s were put out to Neilsons. Nonetheless, it was reported in the *Mechanical World & Steam Users Journal* of September 1885 that in the half year ended 31st July, with a staff of just over 2,000, fourteen new engines had been turned out and 139 repaired; 63 new carriages, 697 repaired and 168 new wagons, 10,687 repaired.

Around 1888 a new paint shop (later retitled Varnish Shop), stores and offices were constructed across the way at the top end of Charles Street and after the turn of the century a private iron foundry was acquired, also in Charles Street. This enabled a survey dated November 1910 (National Railway Museum, BTC paper W136) to state that the site extended to 24 acres, fully 13 acres being roofed, with more than 3,000 staff employed. It was claimed, however, that: 'it is, at this date, barely sufficient for the Company's requirements' but that 'in busy times the workshops can produce in new work annually, 52 engines, 104 carriages and 3,000 wagons.'

In passing, although strictly speaking not part of the main works yet still within the purview of the Locomotive Superintendent, a new four road engine shed was constructed in 1880. This replaced the Running Department's portion

of the G&G works and the cramped two road shed at Buchanan Street. The new establishment, unfortunately, was also less than satisfactory, the shed, turntable and coal stage being strung out on a narrow site at the far end of the works yard, below the Germiston embankment. Accordingly, in November 1916 a mighty twelve road shed plus a two road repair shop was completed just over a mile from the works, beyond the Broomfield Road bridge. Since this was in the Balornock district it attracted that name to itself albeit it was officially entitled St Rollox – something that baffled latter day enthusiasts, especially those from south of the border.

Nothing further of consequence occurred up to the watershed of the grouping except that in the final year the 1,000th new engine was produced, No.431, later LMS 15237, one of a batch of four enlarged 439 class 0-4-4Ts fitted with cast iron buffer beams for banking purposes at Beattock. Pickersgill continued in office for a year but was succeeded by D.C. Urie from the Highland Railway in 1924. It is alleged that he brought a large frame slotting machine with him but its stay was only temporary, for it soon passed on to Crewe. Nonetheless new work continued, twenty 60 class 4-6-0s in 1925/26 and sixty standard class 4F 0-6-0s between 1924 and 1928 but

that was the end; thereafter the works was confined to engine repairs only.

Early after grouping it had been decided that wagon work in the Northern Division should be concentrated on the former G&SWR's relatively modern plant at Barassie and, in due course, this allowed a further reorganisation within St Rollox. Part of the old Wagon Shop became a Carriage Paint Shop and the remainder was taken up by stores and extensions of the Machine and Fitting Shops. Since the engines were painted in the Erecting Shop, the Varnish Shop became simply another storage space.

So far as locomotives were concerned, the Erecting Shop was the centre of activities and A.N. Marshall, while contemplating a railway career, paid a visit on a summer weekend in 1928 (*A Life of Steam*, a previously unpublished autobiography serialised in early volumes of BRILL): *At last we came to the Erecting Shop where I was momentarily disconcerted by the state of déshabillé of 30 or 40 locomotives ranged up and down the two bays. The back of the shop was given over to boilers, but elsewhere pit after pit was occupied by nothing more than a pair of frames, held apart at one end by the cylinder block and at the other end by the drag box with a few cross stays in between. Here and there a boiler would*

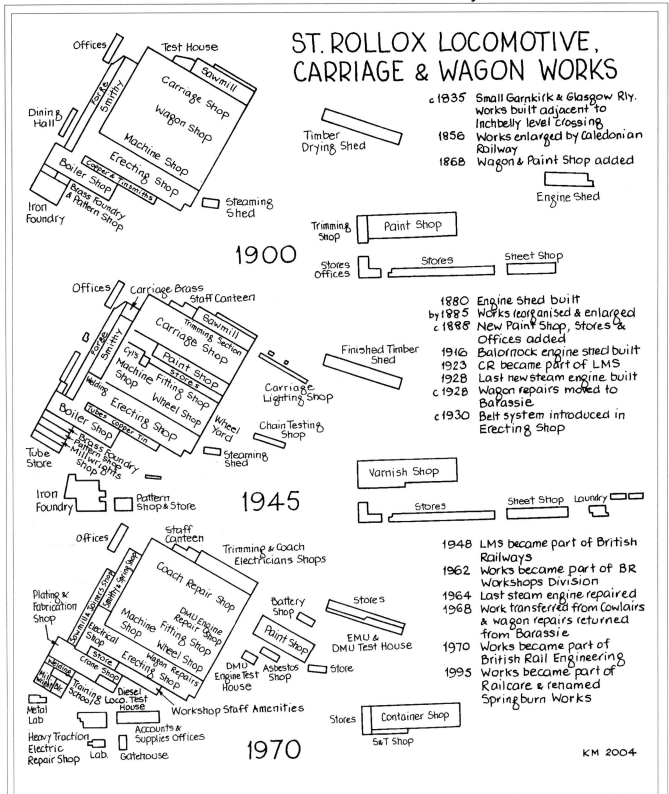

Plans showing the development and changing uses of the works from 1900 to more recent times with a list of significant dates. The original 1945 plan included lots of zigzag lines indicating air raid shelters. At that time the day shift was from 8.00am to 5.00pm but part of the works including the Machine Shop (and the author), Fitting Shop and sections of the Erecting Shop worked a 12 hour night shift, 6.00pm to 6.00am.

be standing close by awaiting installation: there and here frame and boiler conjoined stood ready for wheeling on Monday morning, a set of wheels complete with axleboxes and springs neatly lined up behind, rather like children waiting for the Saturday morning cinema doors to open. Perhaps four or five engines were more or less complete, though lacking their tenders if they happened to possess one, the tenders going through their own regenerative process in the third bay of the shop.

Away down south at Crewe at this time the new '10 Shop' or 'Erecting Shop South' with six pit roads had just been completed with the initiation of the so-called belt system of engine repair. The scheme provided for incoming engines to be stripped on arrival at the rear of the shop and moved back to the doors in stages at predetermined intervals. Dedicated gangs of workmen performed prescribed tasks at each stage. In the final stages, once the engines were mounted on all or some of their wheels, they were coupled with steel cables and moved together like a train. Engines of a similar size were kept to a particular belt and by this means time spent in the shops was reduced to between eight to twelve days. The apparent success

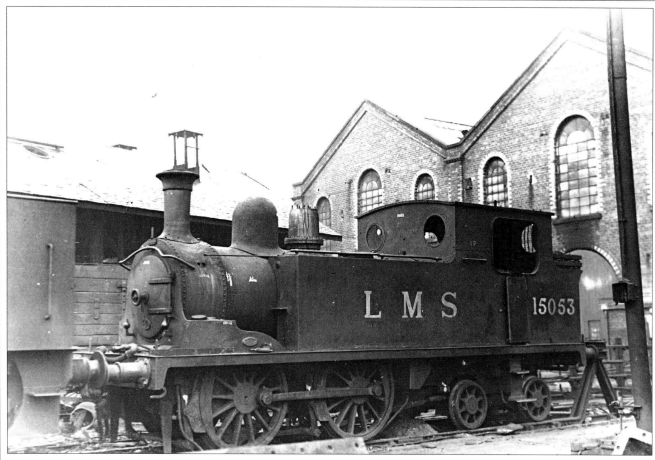

Engines from all the Northern Division pre-grouping companies were dealt with at St Rollox and here, in October 1948, is Highland 'Wick & Lybster' 0-4-4T 15053 arrived for a service repair. Painted plain black it returned to traffic on the Dornoch branch in January 1949 but at its next works visit in June 1955 it received full passenger livery. It was destined to be the last Highland Railway engine in service, withdrawn in January 1957 following a driving axle failure. Photograph: Rex Conway Steam Railway Collection.

of the scheme persuaded management that it should be introduced at other works. It should be said that the coupling together of the engines in the final stages was soon abandoned at Crewe so as to make the system more flexible. As it happens, flexibility was the byword for the set-up at St Rollox, as recorded by A.N. Marshall: *Engines came in at the east end and were lifted about two thirds of the way up the shop to the stripping pits, from which they progressed through the*

various stages of repair down the shop and out again to the steaming shed. Behind the stripping pits minor boiler repairs were carried out. At that time, under the influence of the Crewe belt system, the locomotive bays had just instituted two so-called belts, one in each bay. Casual repairs might be done on the other pit road. The belts were strictly notional and engines moved in fits and starts rather than the more regimented style of Crewe. The aim was, I think, some twelve heavy repairs a week plus a few lights and casuals

and the target time was around twelve working days.

I have in my possession a detailed, but faded copy of 'Drawing No.25952, Locomotive Repair Workshops, St Rollox, Glasgow', signed and dated by D.C. Urie, 13 June 1932. I have redrawn that part depicting the Erecting Shop which, with careful study, reveals the local version of the belt system as described by A.N. Marshall, together with the other activities performed within the shop. Little had changed in the

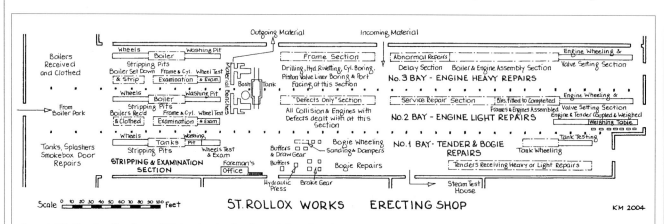

Layout of the Erecting Shop from a 1932 drawing showing the two belts as described by AN. Marshall. The occupation of 3 Bay belt during the July 1946 Glasgow Fair Holiday, starting from the rear of the shop, was: 3F 812 class 0-6-0 17575 collision damage, CR Single 123 cosmetic restoration, Dunalastair IV 4-4-0 14460 heavy repair including new boiler, 2P 439 class 0-4-4T 15235 heavy repair including new boiler and cylinders, Black Five 5178 and Beetlecrusher 0-6-0T 16161 service repairs, 2F Jumbo 0-6-0s 17302 heavy repair and 17300 heavy repair including new boiler. 2 Bay belt comprised Crab 2804, Black Five 5152, 782 class 0-6-0T 16328, 8F 2-8-0 8093 and Black Five 5467 service repairs, Jumbo 0-6-0 17405 heavy repair including new boiler and 4F 0-6-0 4315 heavy repair including change of boiler.

This is the sorry state in which I found CR 123 and HR 103 on my arrival at St Rollox – rusting away outside the Varnish Shop where they'd been since almost the beginning of the war. Eventually they were brought into the Erecting Shop, first the Caley Single in July 1946 then the Jones Goods in September 1947, for cosmetic restoration, ending up in the Carriage Paint Shop. Because of space considerations they were moved back to the Varnish Shop, inside this time, in January 1948. Photograph: James Stevenson.

arrangements by my arrival thirteen years later. Even the foreman was the same – taciturn John Law who personally presided over the positioning of each new arrival in the shop. Rather like the man with the red flag in front of early motor cars, he would pace down the bay followed by the engine slung from the two 50 ton overhead travelling cranes while ensuring that men cleared away from the engines on either side as it passed.

To be honest, I wasn't really aware of a belt system although John Menzies (pronounced Mingers), a fellow engineering apprentice a year senior to me, remembers that there was a big diagram in the Erecting Shop with six pictures of a Black Five in the various stages from just a bare frame to ready to go out of the door and what was supposed to be done at each stage. In 1946, the first full calendar year of my tenure, I recorded all the comings and goings from the time the engines arrived in the yard to their return to service from the steaming shed. In all it averaged 38 programmed repairs and 17 defects and/or others each month. Programmed repairs were

classified as 'Heavy', where the engine was completely dismembered, and 'Service' where, generally speaking, the boiler remained in place. 'Defects' comprised relatively small repairs to specific areas beyond the scope of the home shed – frame weld, L H cylinder rebored, piston valve liners, tyres renewed, are some that I listed but the highest number involved some trouble or other with the boiler. 'Others' mainly comprised collision damage. Throughout the year 633 locomotives passed through the shop with the programmed repairs averaging 12 to 17 days from first arrival to final departure.

All types of Northern Division pre-grouping engines were dealt with, 315 of the 633 in 1946, and all the LMS standards up to the 5XP 'Silver Jubilees'. There was, however, an unexpected visit by 6143 THE SOUTH STAFFORDSHIRE REGIMENT in December 1947 for a service repair, after which it left with its maroon livery cleaned and retouched despite a new post-war black livery having been introduced in 1946. The first engine to receive the latter was 5716 SWIFTSURE in August 1947, applied, unusually in

the Carriage Paint Shop. The only engines to be taken there for painting up to that time had been the cosmetically restored CR 123 and HR 103. Although all new work had stopped with 4F 0-6-0 4476 in 1928, two engines, 16242 and 17603, received new frames in 1946 and twenty-four received new boilers – six LMS standards and the remainder Caledonian. Those for the latter had been fabricated in the works but the others emanated from south of the border.

The last year of my apprenticeship was the first year of the new nationalised British Railways but, apart from the numbers and insignia on the engines leaving the shops, nothing really changed. Towards the end of the year, however, there was an improvement in painting standards. Engines that had received a heavy repair were taken to the Varnish Shop to be given a full paint schedule – three undercoats, one coat enamel and two coats varnish plus lining out for passenger engines of which 55233 was the first at the end of September. Engines were still being lettered BRITISH RAILWAYS at that stage, the lion and wheel emblem not appearing until 54472 in November 1949. Incidentally, in the spirit of togetherness, some LMS engines had begun to be sent to Cowlairs for repair, 17320 being the first in October 1948.

The more recent history of the works can be briefly summarised; in 1962 it became part of the BR Workshops Division with another internal reorganisation to cater for the gradual changeover to diesel traction. The last steam engine to go through the shops was 45213 in 1964. In 1968 Cowlairs closed and the work transferred to St Rollox, followed by that from Barassie and Inverurie thus making it the main BR works in Scotland. Eventually it was retitled 'Glasgow Works'. In 1970 it became part of British Rail Engineering Ltd, was privatised in 1995 and became Railcare's 'Springburn Works'. In its March 26-April 8 1997 issue, *RAIL* was able to report that of twenty-nine main BR workshops repairing locomotives and rolling stock in the early 1960s just six remained and of these only Crewe, Doncaster and Springburn regularly overhauled locomotives. I suppose that could be seen as a sign of success for St Rollox, or should I say The Caley?

****

But who was St Rollox? Well it seems that he was born in Montpellier in 1295 and later achieved fame as a healer of those stricken with the plague, including himself. Veneration of the saint spread across Europe and a chapel in his name was established on common land immediately above Townhead about 1508. For this information I'm again indebted to A.N. Marshall's *A Life of Steam*. Other important reference sources in addition to those already quoted were *An Illustrated History of Glasgow's Railways* (W.A.C. Smith and Paul Anderson, Irwell Press, 1993); *LMS Engine Sheds, Vol. 5, The Caledonian Railway'* (Chris Hawkins, George Reeve and James Stephenson, Wild Swan Publications, 1987; *Life in a Locomotive Works* (Charles Taylor, OPC, 1995); *The Springburn Experience* (Gerard Hutchison and Mark O'Neill, Polygon in association with the Springburn Museum Trust 1989). I'm also beholden to Jim McIntosh, Chairman of the Caledonian Railway Association for his support.

Top right. The site of the 1880 engine shed as viewed from the top of the water tank in May 1948. The array of surplus boilers and other material in wagons, tenders, engines waiting for the shops and withdrawn engines awaiting the torch explains why this area became known as 'The Dump'. During my time the last McIntosh 4-6-0s, the last Highland 'Castles', the last G&SWR engines and many others passed through here – some cut up in the Erecting Shop, others making a funeral procession to Kilmarnock. Photograph: Keith Miles.

Below right. In the early part of 1948 forty-seven engines were turned out with the M prefix. M627 was so dealt with on 10th March and is here seen at Balornock three days later. Three days after that the policy changed in favour of having 40000 added to the numbers. Initially the smokebox number plates were retained but from March 26th they were removed. No new plates were cast until 10th August. Both the cabside numbers and BRITISH RAILWAYS were hand painted. Photograph: James Stevenson.

Below. One of the long-lived Jumbos, 57307, ex-shops in the yard on 14th May 1948. A Drummond engine, it was built at St Rollox as CR 370 in 1887. In 1920 it was given a new boiler with Ross pop safety valves. It had come to the works in May 1946 for attention to the boiler and at that time had tender 1262. On this occasion it left coupled to Lambie tender 971 of 1892 with underslung springs which had been in the Dump for some time. After seventy-three years service it was finally withdrawn in August 1959. Photograph: Keith Miles.

You'll Remember those Black and White Days...

Of the 742 Black Fives running within the former LMS boundaries in mid-1948, 206 were allocated to the Northern Division and maintained at St Rollox. These included the four named after Scottish Territorial Regiments allocated to Balornock. Here's 45157 THE GLASGOW HIGHLANDER fresh from the works at its home shed in May 1948. In April 1957 two of them were transferred to Newton Heath and I was to meet 45156 THE AYRSHIRE YEOMANRY again at Rowsley. This proved to be the last named LMS engine on its withdrawal in August 1968. Photograph: A.G. Ellis.

On 17th May 1948 Black Fives 4998 and 4999 of Perth arrived at the works amid mild speculation since they were fairly new and smartly turned out in the latest LMS post-war livery. Instead of entering the works, however, they were taken to the Varnish Shop and given complete repaints in the new BR black, lined red, cream and grey passenger and mixed traffic livery. Rumours had it that it was in respect of a Royal Train working but I never found the truth of it. Here's 44998 at its home shed later that month. Photograph: The Transport Treasury.

On a visit to the Varnish Shop to see the progress of 44998 and 44999 I came across a raft of carriages destined for the Glasgow-Aberdeen service newly painted in the BR carmine and cream livery. Like the engines they were fairly new, part of a sequence of a hundred 60ft side corridor composite coaches built at Wolverton to diagram 2117 during 1947-48. Were the engines and carriages connected? – perhaps some other septuagenarian has the answer? Photograph: A.G. Ellis.

Now in private hands, the former works offices on Springburn Road in the Glasgow Garden Festival Year 1988. It will be noted, however, that the arched gateway still appears to belong to BREL. The office window beyond the arch was that of Willie Hunter, Superintendent of Apprentices. The Drawing Office, in which I spent my final month, was on the top floor towards the far end. Photograph: Keith Miles.

You'll Remember those Black and White Days...

The passage of 'Packet' or state papers from the Queen to her Lord Lieutenant in Ireland goes back to at least the 1570s and the port of Holyhead played a part in this. By the end of that century, the postal return journey from London to Dublin could be accomplished in a fortnight.

From this small beginning grew 'The Irish Mail' but not without one or two setbacks on the way. Ten years before the railway reached Holyhead, the London-Dublin mails were transferred to travel via Liverpool and it was another ten years before the Admiralty Packet Boat returned to Holyhead. In 1849 the work went out to tender and in the following year went to the Dublin Steam Packet Company, much to the dismay of the Chester & Holyhead Railway Co, whose line had reached Holyhead on 1st August 1848 (but only from Llanfair PG). It was two years later when the Britannia Bridge was completed and through services to 'England' commenced.

In the early years, the location of the embarkation point for Ireland was still not settled, both Holyhead and Porth Dinlleyn on the North Caernarfornshire coast being contenders. The fact that Holyhead was already 'in business' and Stephenson's ability to get a Railway along the North Wales coast and provide bridges to cross the River Conwy and the Menai Strait sealed the matter in favour of Holyhead.

The first station at Holyhead, as in many places, was a temporary one; on the south-west side of what became the later engine shed area. The line was extended to Admiralty Pier on 20th May 1851 – which the 'packet' boats used, and a permanent 'Town' station was provided in September that year, to the west of the present site.

The Admiralty Pier extension was partly on a timber viaduct along the waterfront and was horse worked until about the end of 1859 when, after viaduct strengthening and easement of curves, 0-4-0 tank engines took over.

By 1866 the Quay to the west side of the harbour had been completed and a large good shed provided, replacing one on the Admiralty Pier. This goods shed was used by passengers (other than those using the Irish Mail service). They made use of a platform which was outside the shed wall, fitted with staircases leading to overhead galleries in the

With 'Hibernia' in the background, backed by the station buildings and the Hotel on the far left, loading of the 'Slieve Donard' is underway at the Export Quay in 1960. These will be empty fresh meat 'FM' containers but quite why the one on the chains is labelled 'Geest Bananas' defeats us. See also page 91(top) to set the scene.

HOLYHEAD – THE PORT
A Brief Account by Bryan Wilson

You'll Remember those Black and White Days...

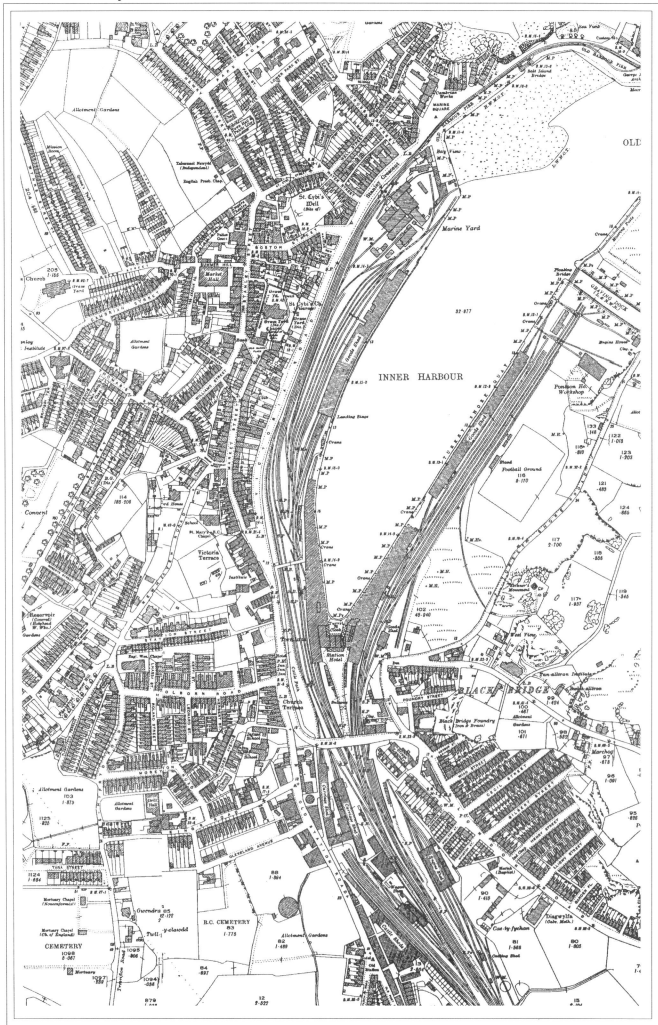

The view from the outside, December 1953. At the bottom of the station approach (reflected in the window) was the Cafeteria with, as it says, an entrance in the concourse. This was a convenient place for staff to park their motor cycles in those pre-car days. These three vintage items date from 1947 (Flintshire), 1950 (Blackpool) and 1952 (East Sussex), not one of them a 'local'. The ironwork above is worth a second look. This is the 1880 (final) station.

goods shed, thence down by further staircases to the quayside. And all this with your luggage, which was quite considerable in those days, as well.

The failure of the London & North Western (who had taken over the Chester & Holyhead) to secure the mail contract when re-tendered in 1870 made the LNW railway company seriously think what to do about their rivals. They decided to commission two new ships, improve the new harbour by dredging and deepening to allow ships to come into the former creek (later the inner harbour) and, above all, to build a new railway station with platforms on two sides of the harbour so that passengers could step almost from train to ship and vice versa. The ship was berthed virtually in part of the station. And, of course, there had to be a new Hotel as well. All this came into use on 17th June 1880 and from the following day, the Greenore and North Wall shipping services used the new station and were 'warped' across from the arrival to

the departure side. A new goods shed on the Up side became the export shed and the old one on the Down dealt with imports which meant that freight movement was exactly opposite that of passengers. Passengers went *out* on the Down side of the harbour and *in* on the Up; freight went out on the Up side of the harbour and came in on the Down. The decision to use the Down side for imports was made because the considerable livestock trade from Ireland had its facilities south of the station on that side and the new arrangement allowed cattle to pass, via their own inclined way and bridge, from 'ship to pen' so to speak.

At last, in 1920, the LNWR won the mail contract from the Dublin Steam Packet Co. The latter had lost the 'Leinster' and the 'Connaught' in the first World War and the fact that Admiralty Pier was no longer as convenient, or as comfortable as the 1880 station played a part, and their last 'mail' sailing left on 27th November 1920. Admiralty Pier

finally closed on 1st April 1925 since which date, all services have used the main station.

Although the inevitable 'rationalisation' of the 1960s affected Holyhead, a container service between London and Eire commenced in January 1968, complete with two new vessels. Progress was interrupted by the Britannia Bridge fire on 23rd May 1970 and it was the end of January 1972 before services returned to normal. Improved car/lorry ferry loading facilities were introduced in 1975/76 and 'roll on, roll off' has since been a very important part of the operations.

The Hotel closed in 1951 and has been demolished whilst the station has been 'modernised', albeit not very sympathetically; it just about gets by for passengers who are generally only 'transient' anyway. Our pictures take a look at the station scene in December 1953 and at shipping operations seven years later.

Table 13

The Irish Mail

EXPRESS SERVICES

LONDON, BIRMINGHAM and MANCHESTER
to
DUBLIN

via HOLYHEAD AND DUN LAOGHAIRE (KINGSTOWN)

TO IRELAND

		DAY SERVICE				NIGHT SERVICE					
		Mondays to Fris.		Saturdays only		Week-nights					R
		am	am	am	am	pm	pm	pm	pm		pm
London (Euston)	dep		8A10		8A10	5A20					8A45
Rugby (Midland)			9 55		9 55	6 57					10 29
Birmingham (New St.)			9C15		9D15	6H24				10M 0	10N10
Crewe			11 35		11 40	8 35				11M24	12a11
Manchester (Exchange)	dep	10A20		10 0		7B10	10F10	10G20			
Warrington (Bank Quay)		11 1		10 41		8B11	10F45	10G55			
Chester (General)	dep	11 35	12p10	11 16	12p15	9 11	11F13	11G45	12M 0		12a46
	arr	1p23	1p45	1p10	1p53	10 51	1F 0	2G 0	1a36		2a25
Holyhead	dep	pm 2 30		pm 2 20		am 3 25					
Dun Laoghaire (Kingstown)	arr	5 45		5 35		6 40					
Dublin (Westland Row)		6 33		6 33		7 23					
(Amiens Street)						7L54					
(Kingsbridge)						8L25					

NIGHT SERVICE (Continued)

		Friday nights Saturday mornings		Sunday nights							
					R						
		pm	am	pm	pm						
London (Euston)	dep		12A50	4K 5	8A45						
Rugby (Midland)				5 50	10 29						
Birmingham (New St.)			11P10	6C35	10C10						
Crewe			4 4	8 25	12a11						
Manchester (Exchange)	dep	11 55		7B25	10A10						
Warrington (Bank Quay)		12a45		7B20	10 45						
Chester (General)	dep	1a35		9 20	11 17	12a46					
	arr	3a35	6 20	11 40	1a 3	2a25					
Holyhead	dep	am 8 15		am 3 25							
Dun Laoghaire (Kingstown)	arr	11 45		6 40							
Dublin (Westland Row)		12 18		7 23							
(Amiens Street)				7 54							
(Kingsbridge)				8 25							

A—Seats may be reserved in advance on payment of a fee of 1s. 0d. per seat. a—am. B—Change at Chester. C—Change at Crewe. D—Change at Crewe, and on Saturdays until 6th Sept. depart Birmingham 9.20 am. F—Runs Fridays and Saturdays only until 19th July then daily. G—Mondays to Thursdays until 17th July. H—Change at Stafford. K—Note A applies. On Sundays until 24th August passengers can depart London (Euston) at 4.40 pm and change at Crewe. L—Except on Sunday mornings. M—Fridays only and runs until 5th Sept. N—Change at Crewe. On Fridays until 5th Sept. departs 10.0 pm by through train. P—Friday nights. Change at Crewe. p—pm. R—Light refreshments available for London to Holyhead passengers. RC—Refreshment Car. SC—1st and 3rd class Sleeping Cars.

NOTICE

3.15 a.m. SAILING HOLYHEAD TO DUN LAOGHAIRE (KINGSTOWN).

Passengers arriving at Holyhead in the early evening may board the vessel at 9.0 p.m.; cabins and berths can be occupied from that hour. Passengers may remain on board after arrival at Dun Laoghaire (Kingstown) until 8.0 a.m. These arrangements may, in exceptional circumstances, have to be cancelled without notice.

For details of Cabins and Berth Charges and addresses to which applications should be made for accommodation on the vessels—see page 43. For details of Steamer Reservation Tickets and general arrangements—see separate folder, to be obtained at Stations and Agencies.

Left and right. TIMETABLE
Summer 1952 Irish Mail service

The view of the Cafeteria from the entrance side. It just proves that 'waiting lounges' are not new and if the weather was adverse, the wait might be longer than you bargained for. The inner harbour is behind us and the careful eye will see a ship reflected in the Cafeteria window. December 1953.

You'll Remember those Black and White Days...

Table 13

Table 13

The Irish Mail
EXPRESS SERVICES
DUBLIN
to
MANCHESTER, BIRMINGHAM and LONDON
Via DUN LAOGHAIRE (KINGSTOWN) AND HOLYHEAD

FROM IRELAND

		DAY SERVICE		NIGHT SERVICE
		Mondays to Fridays am	Saturdays only am	Sunday to Thursday nights pm
Dublin (Kingsbridge)	dep	..	..	7L35
,, (Amiens Street)	,,	..	..	7L56
,, (Westland Row)	,,	7 45	10 0	7 10
Dun Laoghaire (Kingstown)	,,	9 15	11 35	8 40
Holyhead	arr	12p35	2p50	11 55

Holyhead	dep	pm 1A25	pm 4 40	pm 4A50	am 1A10	am 1 25	am 7 10	am 7A30
Chester (General)	arr	2 59	6 20	6 27	5 5 6 55	2 44	3 17	9 36	9 52
Warrington (Bank Quay)	arr	3C50	3 50		7 24	3 53	10 24	
Manchester (Exchange)	arr	4C31	4 31		8 5	4 27	11 3	
Crewe	,,	3 33		7 3	3 20	5G33	10 31
Birmingham (New St.)	,,	5D27	4 8		4 55		12D50
Rugby (Midland)	,,	5D16	8 27 9D21		6 30		1D16
London (Euston)	,,	6 35	10 10				1p32

NIGHT SERVICE (continued)

		Friday nights pm	Saturday nights pm	Saturday nights commencing 12th July pm
Dublin (Kingsbridge)	dep	7 35	7 35	..
,, (Amiens Street)	,,	7 56	7 56	..
,, (Westland Row)	dep	7 10	7 10	9 25
Dun Laoghaire (Kingstown)	,,	8 40	8 40	10 45
Holyhead	arr	11 55	11 55	2a15

Holyhead	dep	am 1A45	am 2 0	am 7 10	am 7A30	am 1A45	am 2 0	am 3A45	am 4 0
Chester (General)	arr	3 22	3 52	9 43	9 52	3 22	3 52	5 22	5 52
Warrington (Bank Quay)	,,		4 6	10 27			4 35		6 28
Manchester (Exchange)	,,		5 10	11 15			5 10		7 9
Crewe	arr	4 6		10 31		4 6		5 58	
Birmingham (New St.)	,,	6D50		12D50		6D50		8D21	
Rugby (Midland)	,,	5 36		12D49		5 36			
London (Euston)	,,	7 20		1p27		7 20		9 7	

A—Seats may be reserved in advance on payment of a fee of 1s. 0d. per seat. a—am. C—Change at Chester. Applies until 18 July only. D—Change at Crewe. G—Change at Crewe and on Mondays arrive Birmingham 6.50 am. L—Except on Sundays. p—pm. RC—Refreshment Car. SC—1st and 3rd class Sleeping Cars. T—Light Refreshments available. TC—Through Carriages.

NOTICE
8.40 pm SAILING—DUN LAOGHAIRE (KINGSTOWN) TO HOLYHEAD.

Passengers may board the vessel at Dun Laoghaire (Kingstown) at 7.30 pm; cabins and berths can be occupied from that hour. Passengers may remain on board after arrival at Holyhead until 8.0 am. except on Saturday and Sunday mornings, when this facility is not available.
These arrangements may, in exceptional circumstances, have to be cancelled without notice.

For details of Cabins and Berth Charges and addresses to which applications should be made for accommodation on the vessels—see page 43. For details of Steamer Reservation Tickets and general arrangements—see separate folder, to be obtained at Stations and Agencies.

40

The passengers arrive, and they certainly did, in bulk sometimes, with up to 26 trains during a peak summer night connecting with the two sailings each way on offer. No less than five staff in view here, one in the carriage doorway with the inevitable 'paperwork' that always seemed to pass from person to person; two are looking for a 'tip' job and one views the camera with suspicion. Little Johnny has been told to put the things that he played with on the train into the bag and his brother has to carry his own overcoat. Fine detail here of the drop window in the carriage door – with leather strap – and mails can be seen through the barred window. It must be an 'Extra' – from the weather damage to carriage roof, it looks as if it has been stabled somewhere for a while. December 1953.

You'll Remember those Black and White Days...

The race is on! Down the platform and onto the ship. 1950s clothing par excellence – and school caps *will* be worn.

Nocturne on the concourse December 1953. The ship and the passengers have gone and the place is almost eerie. Just two cups on the window sill tell us that a couple of passengers left their drinks until the last minute.

The wider view. Still no passengers on this wet night but the posters reflect the 'international' flavour of the place. London, Belgian Cities, Coleraine and Wells. The ornamental ironwork shows up well against the lit up balcony windows. The ticket collector's box is a fine example of the species. The man here would deal with passengers to and from the town. The inspection for boat passengers was made between train and gangplank.

Turning round to face west, the rear coach of the last arrival can be seen in Platform One. It is in the red and cream livery of the time. The Refreshment Room has just one customer, or is it a member of staff? Eventually, the Room and the Cafeteria were replaced by just one facility.

The train has gone, the Refreshment Room has closed its doors and all is quiet. The building to the right is the Telegraph Office. The electric cable to the 'Cafeteria' sign looks a bit vulnerable.

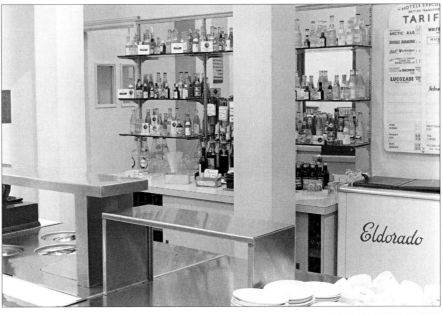

Inside the 'filling station' was a host of goodies and as they would say 'A wide selection of drinks'. 1/9d for a gin or just 1/5d for a bottle of Worthington would go down well and 'Lucozade' is just 10d for a small bottle. Cigarettes on display include 'Piccadilly' and 'Kensitas'. 'Phensic' is available for those who partake of too much of the liquid on offer. Proper cups and saucers and an 'Eldorado' ice cream cabinet complete the display.

Star of the show SS 'Cambria' in 1960. Launched by Harland & Wolff, Belfast on 21st September 1948 and completed May 1949 for the Holyhead-Dun Laoghaire route. She could carry 2,360 passengers in two classes. In the 1967 Register, she weighed in at 5,284 tons gross. She passed to Saudi Arabia in 1976 for £350,000 and was renamed 'ALTAIF' – and eventually sank at her moorings off Suez. 'Cambria' and sister ship 'Hibernia' were the first vessels to be built under the British Transport Commission regime.

The 'relief' ship to the Cambria and Hibernia was the 'Princess Maud'. She was built by William Denny & Bros Ltd, Dumbarton and weighed in at 2,917 gross tons. Although the faster of the three ships, she was also rather 'playful' on anything less than calm seas. Passengers were a bit apprehensive as they boarded the 'Maud' and it is said that the ships crews regarded her 'with a fondness similar to that shown to a mischievous child'. She was withdrawn from service in September 1965 and left Holyhead for a refit at Brest on 17th of that month en route to Greek waters. Our view in December 1960 shows her on the departure side in Holyhead Inner Harbour with St Cybi's Church behind – hence Holyhead = Caergybi.

To help get your bearings. 'Slieve Donard' is ahead of us alongside the Export Quay in 1960 and 'Hibernia' (seen on page 82) across at the passenger departure Quay. The Export Shed is straight ahead beneath the gantry crane. 'Slieve Donard' is only nine months old in this October 1960 view. She replaced her namesake on the Holyhead-Dublin (North Wall) route and is specially fitted out for unit loads, cattle and vehicles. She can cope with 685 beasts, 639 tons of cargo and 63 containers. She can carry 100 cars driven on, at the stern. There is no passenger accommodation. The two masts positioned amidships leave the decks clear for cargo. She left Holyhead on 1st July 1976 after sale to Jeddah, Saudi Arabia and survived until 1987.

Nocturne on the Export Quay, 1960. Just 'Slieve Donard' and a duty officer guarding his packages.

You'll Remember those Black and White Days...

The view from the Export Quay across the Inner Harbour to the Marine Department's Yard on the west side, October 1960. The line to Admiralty Pier ran behind these buildings and a couple of wagons can be seen to the left of the crane cab on the causeway to Salt Island.

The rail to ship connection in the Export Shed, October 1960. Containers are aboard round the deck of the 'Slieve Donard', including another labelled 'Bananas'. All the impedimenta of the Quayside, barrels, ropes, slings, hooks, chains, barrows and trolleys of all sorts.

The loaded train takes shape; containers have now been separated from general goods vehicles. Note the crossover lines within the shed for ease of marshalling.

As Holyhead sleeps, 'Slieve Donard' now cleared of traffic waits to cross to the Export side for yet another load to North Wall.

Thanks to Martin Smith and his shipping friends for their help.

You'll Remember those Black and White Days...

Shed A Tear

A sad end for Bulleid Pacifics in South Wales yards in 1968, months after the end of steam on the Southern. Perhaps the most striking picture is presented by 34102, once LAPFORD, looking rather like the specially sectioned Bulleid for the the National Railway Museum, at Buttigieg's yard. A perfect view of boiler tubes and the arrangement of stays in the firebox crown. Of particular interest is the item in the right foreground – a chunk of locomotive mainframe with spring and axlebox still within the frame and with flexible oil feed pipe still intact. With the axlebox also intact, the axle must have been torched/cut through so that it fell out! Photograph The Transport Treasury.

34036 had once been WESTWOOD HO but by the winter of 1968 was languishing in Cashmore's, Newport. A long and dismal procession made its way along this siding for 'processing' into lumps for melting down – a few months after this it was the turn of a couple of the original NB D600 Warships – BULLDOG and COSSACK. Photograph The Transport Treasury.

34040, CREWKERNE that was, at Cashmore's at the same time. Note how the rods have been stowed in the firebox for the final journey. Photograph The Transport Treasury.

The cutter's tale. It was desperately hard, noisy and dirty work, and accidents must have been a constant hazard, you suspect. There were flares from pockets of accumulated grease and oil and you had to keep an eye out for the way components might fall after the cutting – and this was before the menace of asbestos was even dreamed of. Photograph The Transport Treasury.

You'll Remember those Black and White Days...

Endpiece...

You'll Remember those Black and White Days...